OLD FURNITURE

Understanding the Craftsman's Art

SECOND, REVISED EDITION

BY NANCY A. SMITH

DRAWINGS BY GLENNA LANG
PHOTOGRAPHS BY RICHARD CHEEK
except as otherwise noted

DOVER PUBLICATIONS, INC.
New York

To my family,
which has been cajoled, bribed, badgered
and resigned into endurance

ACKNOWLEDGMENTS

SO MANY PEOPLE HAVE SHOWN interest in this book, having extended encouragement and enthusiasm for its success over the years. The isolated long-ago cheers I still recall, and I thank each again—each knows who he is. In turn, I cheer on the readers of this book in hopes that it will add to their discrimination, rewards and pleasure in the pursuit and study of old furniture.

The continuing implementation of this book has been assisted by consultation, patience and energies of many more people. I thank them herewith for their generosity:

Mr. Arthur C. Alexander, Royall House; Ms. Pauline Allaway; Mrs. Georgia Bumgardner, American Antiquarian Society; Ms. Beth Carver; the late Mr. Vincent Cerbone, Museum of Fine Arts, Boston; Mr. Richard Cheek; Mrs. Paul Coombs; Mrs. John Demers; Mr. and Mrs. Edward Dewey; Ms. Deborah Emerson; Mr. Jonathan Fairbanks and Mr. Edward S. Cooke, Jr., Museum of Fine Arts, Boston; Ms. Etta Falkner, Sturbridge Village; The Gibson House Museum, Boston; Ms. Kathryn Gill, The Metropolitan Museum of Art, New York; Ms. Katherine C. Grier, The Strong Museum, Rochester; Mrs. James Hamill; Mr. Henry Harlow, Sturbridge Village; Mr. R. Bruce Hoadley, University of Massachusetts, Amherst; Mr. Brock Jobe and Mr. Richard Nylander, The Society for the Preservation of New England Antiquities; Ms. Patricia Kane, Garvin Collection, Yale University; Ms. Myrna Kaye; Ms. Glenna Lang; Mrs. Maha Maklad; Mr. John W. Melody, Winterthur Museum; Ms. Dorothy Monroe; Ms. Rosalie Moretti; Mr. Marvin Moss, Thonet Industries, Inc.; Mr. Robert D. Mussey, Jr.; Mrs. Ruth Nickerson; Mrs. J. Clifford Ross; Ms. Ellen Rosenthal; Ms. Barbara Neilson Shafto; Mr. Lawrence Sickman, William Rockhill Nelson Gallery of Art; Ms. Jane Tucker, Castle Tucker, Wiscasset, Maine; Dr. and Mrs. Joseph Vargas; Mr. Bron Warsaskas; Mr. Marc A. Williams; Mr. Michael Wilson, Victoria and Albert Museum, London; Wu Tung, Museum of Fine Arts, Boston.

Published in Canada by General Publishing Company, Ltd., 30 Lesmill Road, Don Mills, Toronto, Ontario.

Published in the United Kingdom by Constable and Company, Ltd., 3 The Lanchesters, 162–164 Fulham Palace Road, London W6 9ER.

This Dover edition, first published in 1991, is a revised and enlarged republication of the work originally published by the Bobbs-Merrill Company, Inc., Indianapolis, 1975 (corrected printing published by Little, Brown and Company, Boston, 1976). For the Dover edition the author has updated the text and written an entirely new chapter (Chapter 14, "Upholstery").

Manufactured in the United States of America
Dover Publications, Inc., 31 East 2nd Street, Mineola, N.Y. 11501

Library of Congress Cataloging-in-Publication Data

Smith, Nancy A.
    Old furniture : understanding the craftsman's art / by Nancy A. Smith ; drawings by Glenna Lang ; photographs by Richard Cheek. — 2nd, rev. ed.
        p.   cm.
    Includes bibliographical references and index.
    ISBN 0-486-26339-8 (pbk.)
    1. Furniture making. 2. Furniture—Repairing. 3. Furniture finishing. I. Lang, Glenna. II. Cheek, Richard. III. Title.
TT194.S63   1991
749'.1—dc20   90-41037
                                                                                  CIP

For the material on reparation of tables on pages 123 and 124, the author is indebted to Charles H. Hayward's *Furniture Repairs*, published by Evans Brothers, Ltd., London, 1967.

CONTENTS

INTRODUCTION

OLD FURNITURE IS EXCITING. Richness of wood figure combined with the mellowness of age have tremendous emotional appeal to most viewers in this age of bustle, space and synthetics. One senses that each old piece is unique, made for one person by another in a time and life-style that we do not know, cannot recapture and thus hold in reverence.

The cabinetmaker of today rarely has the opportunity to create from the magnificent pieces of hardwood used in the past—splendid, huge, richly figured boards, measuring up to three feet in width. An entire 18th-century tea-table top was frequently made from a single piece of wood. Fine wood such as mahogany, imported from the Caribbean, and used by the cabinetmaker for his best work, was as important a part of 18th-century Elegance as the tea and silk imported from the Orient. Even today we can sense and participate in the pleasure the use of the finest materials gave both craftsman and customer alike.

Old furniture is exciting in its design and detail. Which designs and which details most appeal to each individual becomes personal preference but certainly all have been admired in each generation. The fact that furniture reproduction, faking and the search for the truly old have flourished to the extent that they have during the 19th and 20th centuries indicates the general attraction of old pieces.

A further source of admiration today is the tremendous skill and resourcefulness of yesterday's furniture craftsman working by hand in his shop with hand tools. Occasionally an available furniture-design book would suggest ideas and styles, sometimes seeing pieces which had been made elsewhere would alter his planning and encourage new skills, certainly patrons dictated wishes, but each furniture maker in the end made his own contribution. Consider the cabinetmaking skill involved in the creation of this card-table top (illustration 2) with a rounded corner recessed for candlesticks and an oval pocket for chips, the whole accomplished with a single piece of wood as can be seen by following the continuous wood grain. Because of details employed by certain cabinetmakers, it is possible to recognize, categorize and regionalize individuals and groups of cabinetmakers (the Townsend-Goddard family in Newport, for example). These many combined skills, impressively mastered (or not), brought the piece into being, and we admire and seek out the products of the early cabinetmaker's abilities—something almost gone in our assembly-line society.

1

1. Interior of the Dominy Woodworking Shop, East Hampton, New York, now reconstructed at the Winterthur Museum, where the Dominy family of craftsmen worked from about 1760 to about 1840. The cabinetmaker's oak workbench here seen was the center of his activity. Photograph courtesy The Henry Francis du Pont Winterthur Museum.

2. Rounded corner of mahogany Boston card-table top interior, ca. 1730–1750.

A fascinating aspect of old furniture is its history. One can speculate upon who made a particular piece for whom and for what reason or occasion. The circumstances through which a piece has survived to be with us today provoke the imagination. Sometimes it is possible to learn such details by checking family records and doing other kinds of research.

The excitement of old furniture becomes even greater when one recognizes the furniture details and techniques that have come down to us through history. How interesting to realize that the mortise-and-tenon joint was utilized in Old Kingdom Egypt, ca. 2600 B.C. This is documented by the study of the gold-cased bed canopy, now in the Cairo Museum, found in the tomb of Queen Hetepheres I, mother of Cheops, builder of the Great Pyramid. The Egyptian chair with animal legs and a sloping back (illustration 4), one of the oldest existing chairs, dating from the XVIIIth Dynasty (ca. 1570–1320 B.C.), is also constructed with mortise-and-tenon joints and is fastened with visible pegs.

Earliest Chinese chair and table construction (about 800 A.D., before which the Chinese used mats on the floor) display traditional construction and jointing. No furniture remains extant prior to the 15th century, so

3. Old Kingdom Egypt mortise-and-tenon joint from bed canopy of Queen Hetepheres I, showing copper-cased mortise and tenon forming practical bearing surfaces. Photograph courtesy the Museum of Fine Arts, Boston.

4. New Kingdom Egypt cedar wood chair with bone and ivory inlays. Photograph courtesy the Brooklyn Museum, Charles Edwin Wilbour Fund.

Introduction · 3

5. *Fifteenth-century Kang table of huang-hua li wood (a variety of rosewood) with cabriole legs. Height, 12″; length, 36⅜″; depth, 23″. Photographs courtesy private collection.*

pictured here (illustrations 5 and 6) are a 15th-century Chinese table and an early 17th-century chair of the Ming Dynasty (1368–1644 A.D.). The table shows the use and appreciation of hardwood for furniture at this early date. Not only was such wood considered beautiful but its hardness and strength allowed designs to be light and graceful. The cabriole leg with the scrolled foot, for example, so universal to 18th-century cabinetwork, dates back at least to Tang Dynasty China (618–907 A.D.). The Chinese also veneered core wood with finer wood sheets of veneer. Note the panel and frame seat construction using mitre-corner mortise-and-tenon joints on the Ming Dynasty chair. The chair's back with contoured splat and the horseshoe-shaped continuous rail were an important influence in early 18th-century European furniture design.

Proof of the excitement of old furniture can be found in the marketplace. Any marketplace is intriguing, and the market for old furniture grows increasingly dynamic. Old pieces, genuine to their period of history, are highly prized and desired. Given the limited supply and the growing demand, the values and prices paid for ownership continue to rise. This can be clearly seen by visiting antique shops, auction sales and antique shows, as well as by studying the specialized publications. A particularly challenging aspect of the old-furniture market is the presence of spurious pieces. The question of faking and how to look for authenticity in an "old" piece will be dealt with at length in this text.

As increasing numbers of people become interested in old furniture, information on how to recognize and judge a given piece would seem very welcome in assisting the new student and collector to appreciate old pieces and buy wisely. During my apprenticeship experience with a cabinetmaker working with old tools in the traditional ways, he encouraged me to explore and discern more and new aspects of old furniture. I come to you with my discoveries up to now, and I hope that they will be helpful and interesting to you as they have been to me.

In the following pages, attempts will be made to train and sharpen the reader's powers of observation and deduction—thereby enabling him to best recognize the most important rudimentary qualities and features pertinent to handcrafted furniture of wood. We shall analyze many aspects of furniture construction—the interior vs. the exterior of a piece, panelling and moldings, the major joints and where each is used, old nails and screws, the intricacies of wood carving, the significance of planing

marks and details of veneering. Furniture finishes will also be examined.

A study of wood movement will be made and its telltale signs of movement with time will be investigated. Contrary to much thinking, wood is in a constant state of change regardless of age—it expands and contracts with temperature and humidity changes and it reacts differently depending on the kind and part of the wood used.

Another section of this book will be devoted to the accessories of furniture—its brasses, hinges, locks, castors and glass. These are vital parts of any piece, functional as well as decorative, and provide many clues to the history of a piece. Often they are a source of delight in their creativity, and it is good fun to discover how flamboyant the craftsman could be. In the approach to these accessories, the importance of considering both sides of any given object will be stressed. Although this is not always easy to do—locks, for example, are securely embedded in old wood—such study can supply critical information when a piece of furniture falls under suspicion.

In addition to the physical properties of old furniture

6. *Seventeenth-century Ming Dynasty Continuous Horseshoe Chinese armchair of huang-hua li wood. Courtesy of Robert Hatfield Ellsworth, from his book "Chinese Furniture" (Random House, New York).*

Introduction · 5

and how it was made, old pieces shall be considered in terms of what has happened to them with time. A chapter on points of wear examines the aging process and its effects on furniture (sometimes to the extent of actual damage). A chapter will deal with furniture repairs—what repairs and restorations can teach us about the history of a piece and how to identify and evaluate such work.

Once the basic principles of old-furniture identification are understood, further refinements and details must be researched and mastered. That is to say, after a piece has been considered in terms of its age characteristics, its construction and condition, attention should be directed to judging the piece as a good representative of its period in terms of style, proportion, material and detail. Provenance is another interesting consideration. Emotion also plays a role. Opinions vary as to the priority of these various factors.

Weighing these many considerations is an exercise which will improve with repetition and experience, the so-called training of a "good eye." There are also the preservation responsibilities, including conservation ethics, to be addressed with awareness and planning. Historic furniture today is viewed as aesthetic, historic and cultural documents, and collectors and curators are temporary keepers and guardians of these surviving artifacts.

Part **I**

FURNITURE-MAKING TECHNIQUES

Chapter **1**

Wood: Its Characteristics and How It Is Worked

MAN'S EARLIEST FURNITURE, known to us by its remains or through pictorial data, was made of wood. This is not surprising since wood was readily available, possible to work with the simplest of tools, and served the intended purposes. Furniture construction as such had its beginning when the woodworker ceased making chests by hollowing out tree trunks and making the lids from one thick plank, and instead began banding individual boards with wrought-iron straps and hinging the lids. These hewn chests, predating the 15th century, are the earliest examples of Western furniture in existence today.

As more tools were developed to aid the woodworker and his understanding of his materials increased, stout planks either split or sawn from the log were crudely put together with oak pins or wrought-iron nails at the angles. In the 16th and 17th centuries, chests were joined with joints, such as the mortise-and-tenon joint, and the woodworker involved was called a joiner.

The chest was the earliest form of what we call case furniture today. This category of furniture suggests a case or box kind of construction. Other case pieces include chests of drawers, cabinets, cupboards, desks and sideboards. The other main categories of furniture are chair furniture (including settees and sofas) whose considera-tions and methods of construction are completely different from case pieces, and table furniture, again having unique construction requirements.

All of these many forms of furniture first became prevalent in the late 17th century, and many skills were required of the maker—far beyond the simple jointing of heavy solid wood pieces by the joiner of earlier days. Hence, the "cabinetmaker" became a highly respected craftsman and the names of many are still known today. His skills included jointing, veneering, turning, carving and finishing the wood. He used both local woods and woods from distant lands which had different properties or were fashionably pleasing.

There are a great many varieties of wood, a number of which have been used in the construction and decoration of furniture. As we have noted, the earliest furniture of the West in existence today in any quantity is of hand-hewn riven oak (i.e., split on its natural cleavage lines with an axe or adze) and dates back to the 15th and 16th centuries. These pieces have survived because oak was available everywhere to be used as a construction material and was so used, and because good quality oak is especially strong and durable.

7. *Thirteenth-century Rhineland coffer of hand-hewn oak planks.*

In the 17th, 18th and 19th centuries, certain woods became fashionable and appropriate for use by cabinet-makers in the making of furniture. One of these was walnut which, with its interesting natural figures, color and decorative burls, contributed to the fashion of veneered furniture during the late 17th and early 18th centuries.

When the West Indies mahoganies were discovered and imports became possible, this close-grained strong wood lent itself well to the rococo carving and fretwork which became popular during the careers of cabinet-makers such as Chippendale and Shearer in the mid-18th century. The earliest mahoganies adopted and worked, about 1730, were dark and heavy woods without figure and they were worked in the solid. Other mahoganies were finely figured, some with great exuberant plume figures, and thus, veneer furniture construction was again practiced.

Toward the end of the 18th century, carving as decoration was replaced by veneers of various woods and inlaid designs. New and exotic woods for veneer work were introduced, many of which were imported from foreign lands. For example, satinwood, much of it from the West Indies, was used more at this time than ever before or since. The style of Hepplewhite and the designs of the Adam Brothers are representative of this so-called "Age of Satinwood."

Ubiquitous pine, a softwood, was used during these same years as both a primary wood (wood that shows) and as a secondary wood (wood parts not intended to be seen, such as the core wood to which decorative veneer is glued). Other local woods, both hardwoods and softwoods, were used for furniture construction. The varie-

ties are endless, but poplar, maple, cherry, beech, fruitwoods, chestnut, ash and yew are frequently encountered. Because of the practicality of using the immediately available, relatively cheap, and familiar local wood, the study of regional woods becomes an interesting method for identifying the geographical area in which a piece of furniture might have been made. Unfortunately, however, wood was sometimes traded between areas, so that any conclusion at best is speculative. Furthermore, it is extremely difficult many times to decide with certainty what the wood really is. Microscopic examination of the cell structure of a piece of wood can usually determine the genus to which it belongs and, in many cases, the species; specialized laboratories for this analysis include the Forest Products Laboratory in Madison, Wisconsin. Use of local wood for furniture making usually goes hand in hand with solid-wood construction (rather than veneer work) and designs of relative simplicity, as compared to high-fashion urban pieces made at the same time.

Certain woods, with their own characteristics and properties, influenced styles at different periods of history. And in reverse, the requirements of different fashions and needs brought individual woods into use and prominence. Thus, the Queen Anne style is often referred to as the "Age of Walnut" while the "Age of Mahogany" is synonymous with mid-18th-century Georgian and American Colonial furniture. In broad terms this proves a helpful initial approach to identifying furniture. A Chinese Chippendale chair carved in oak, for example, would indeed be a rarity—certainly requiring careful scrutiny before confirmation.

8. *Late 18th-century bow-front chest of drawers with drawer fronts of matched plume-figured mahogany veneer.*

9. *English knife box of satinwood veneer, circa 1780, with decorative over-painting and inlay bandings of rare woods.*

Wood: Its Characteristics and How It Is Worked · 11

a.

b.

10. *Wood-grain variations:*

a. A log cut from different angles causes the straight-grain appearance to vary.

b. A curved log cut straight produces wood grain of parabola figure.

c. Branches grow from the pith at the center of the tree, deflecting the direction of the grain, which appears as knots when the board is sawn.

c.

WOOD GRAIN

Straight Grain

All wood has grain. Grain refers to the direction and arrangement of the wood elements—the longitudinal cells, which include vessels, tracheids and fibers. The natural development of the fibrous elements, sometimes called tracheid vessels, in relation to the axis of growth, results in grain. When the general direction of the elements parallels the direction of growth (from bottom to top of trunk) the grain is *straight grain.* (See illustration 10 for examples of wood-grain variations.)

Irregular Grain

Due to knots and other irregularities in the wood, deflections occur in the growth of the wood elements, producing *irregular grain.* Other natural causes may alter the straight grain growth, resulting in *wavy grain* (horizontal waves), which is sometimes produced in the limb area where reaction occurs as the tree trunk and branches expand in their seasonal growths; genetics may also be a consideration. *Spiral grain,* when the elements twist, *interlocked grain,* when the elements of successive growth rings twist in alternate directions as they grow upward, and *silver grain,* which contains flecks or broader and longer markings produced by wood rays, are other ramifications.

Smooth and Rough Grain

In addition to its character and direction, grain may be either smooth or rough depending on whether the fibers have remained flat and unbroken in the cutting and planing of the wood or whether they have lifted and frayed during these operations. Also, the grain fiber of some woods is naturally larger than others; ash, for example, despite flat and unbroken fibers would require filling with composition to achieve a smooth surface (review page 88).

End Grain

Reference should also be made here to the term "end grain." End grain refers to the opened longitudinal cells (tracheids in softwoods and vessels in hardwoods) caused when a cut is made across the log, i.e., a cut perpendicular to the direction of the grain. As we shall see in Chapter 9, end-grain wood behaves differently from long-grain wood and consequently involves special treatment on the part of the cabinetmaker.

11. Bisected wood crotch showing disturbed wood grain at the fork.

12. Swirl crotch figure.

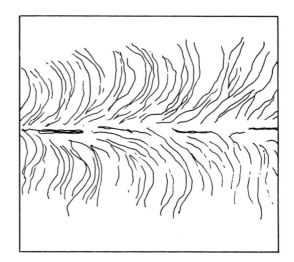

13. Feather or plume figure.

WOOD FIGURE

Figure is the natural design or pattern seen on the surface of a given cut board or wood surface. This pattern should not be confused with the grain of the wood. Figure is brought out by cutting timbers so that veneers or solid surfaces display various kinds of irregularities in cell shape and angle, variations in color, and other internal effects. The manner in which the log is cut can be tangential, plain, radial or quarter sawed. (See illustration 21.) There are many kinds and examples of figure.

Crotchwood Figure

This figure, especially examples in mahogany, is probably the most dramatic and universally exploited type of figure for veneer. It is formed below the point where a tree trunk forks into two large branches resulting from distortions in the elements of growth. It is apparent in the figuring of tangentially cut veneers. The spreading direction of the elements appears as inverted arcs forming what is known as swirl crotch figure. When the veneer cuts reach the point of the crotch, where the greatest stress and compression has occurred, a feather figure or plume-like formation penetrates or divides the swirl figure. It is interesting to note that feather or swirl crotch veneers were usually laid upon vertical surfaces with the grain running in the opposite direction to that which it takes in the tree.

14. Fiddle-back figure as seen in a radially cut log.

15. Curly or "tiger" figure.

Fiddle-Back Figure

Fiddle-back derives from wavy grain. The markings, resembling ripples, are brought out by cutting through the crests of successive undulations in the grain fibers, and they are best shown when the surface has been cut radially from the source. Mahogany, maple and sycamore trees are likely timbers for this figure.

Curly Figure

Especially associated with so-called tiger maple, curly figure is sometimes derived from the irregularities of the wood-grain elements at the bases of large branches. Tiger figure can also be found in parts of the tree where growth has not been affected by branches; genetics is thus suggested as a possible source for this figure. It is displayed in wavy line markings and sometimes curls. However, these horizontal figures are less delicate and more erratic than fiddle-back patterns. Curly figure can be seen on the drawer fronts of the highboy shown in illustration 220, page 154.

Oyster Figure

This figure comes from circular or elliptical patterns displayed by the concentric growth rings in thin cross sections, or diagonally cut sections of branches. These sections are known as oyster pieces, and parquetry panels of oyster veneer on table surfaces and cabinet doors were very fashionable in 17th-century England.

Burl Figure

The veneers sliced from burls—excrescences found growing on the trunks of various trees—contain tiny knot-like markings or eyes. A curly grain and thus figure appears, often forming loops around the knotty eyes. The burl veneers of walnut and elm are the best known for furniture use (the confused cell structure makes the particular species difficult to identify). Notice the Queen Anne dressing-table top shown in Illustration 138, page 94. The greatest density of burl figure is most desirable, whether the burl is used for veneer or turned as a bowl in the solid.

16. Oyster figure.

17. *Burl figure.*

18. *Tree trunk showing burl.*

Bird's-Eye Figure

Bird's-eye figure is apparently caused by a fungus that attacks some North American and European maple trees, resulting in brownish specks which extend through several layers of growth rings. The wood is tangentially sawed, bringing out the figure by cutting through the specks, which are found in irregular or circular, almost crater-like markings.

Growth-Ring Figure

Perhaps the most obvious and basic figure, this is produced in plain-sawed wood cut through the annual layers (or rings) of timbers. The marked differences which occur in the wood substance developed during the early and late periods of each growing season appear as stripes, parabolas and ellipses. Oak, chestnut, ash and elm have very conspicuous marking of this type. Examples of growth-ring figure appear in illustrations 10 and 20.

19. *Bird's-eye figure.*

20. *Parabola growth-ring figure.*

a.

b.

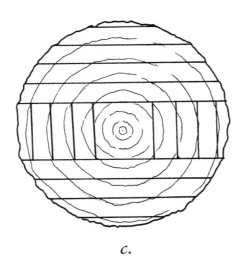

c.

21. *Wood conversion into boards:*

a. Plain-sawn log. Boards cut at edge, most tangential, have straight growth-ring figure; those cut through the heart have full growth-ring figure.

b. Quarter- or radial-cut log. All boards have full figure, are less liable to warp and are stronger.

c. Tangential-cut log or boxed-heart log. No part of the heart appears on any board.

d. End section of plain-sawn log.

e. End section of quartered board.

d.

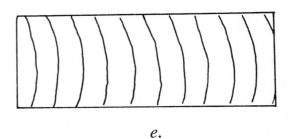

e.

CUTTING OF THE WOOD

Regardless of furniture style and form or kind of wood used, it has always been necessary to begin by cutting logs into boards. (Consider some of the conversions here illustrated.) Due to the plentiful wood supply, only the largest trees were felled in the early 18th century, thereby providing wonderfully wide boards for use in furniture making. (Some of the largest 18th-century tea-table tops measure 31″ and 35″ in diameter, the top all one board.) When narrow planks—18″ or less—are detected in an early piece, it can be an indication of the use of wood of later introduction. (See gateleg table, illustration 168, page 116.) Tools for cutting were simple, and signs of their use remain in evidence on a finished piece of furniture—an excellent guide for establishing authenticity.

The Pit Saw

The early pit saw was not conducive to producing timber of perfect "standard size," although it was amazingly accurate. The boards will vary slightly in width and thickness, despite a cabinetmaker's efforts to minimize these differences by subsequent planing and sawing. If early 18th-century boards are measured they will show discrepancies in size.

A Sawyer.

22. *Cutting timber with the pit saw. (Engraving,* The Book of English Trades and Library of the Useful Arts, *London, 1827.) The man at the top controlled the line of the two-handed saw and was called the top sawyer; the man in the pit merely supplied energy. Photograph courtesy the American Antiquarian Society.*

23. *Back side of 17th-century desk box showing angled, straight, parallel kerf marks from the pit saw.*

24. *Mr. Smart's circular-saw mill with continuous rotary-blade cutting appeared in print as early as 1816 in* A New and Complete Dictionary of Arts and Sciences Including the Latest Improvement and Discovery and the Present State of Every Branch of Human Knowledge *by George Gregory (Isaac Pierce, Philadelphia, 1816). Photograph courtesy the American Antiquarian Society.*

Saw Kerf Marks

The saw marks made by the blade of the pit saw, known as saw kerf marks, are long, straight, parallel marks, slightly angled. When the totally manual pit saw was replaced by the man- or water-powered rip saw in the middle of the 18th century, the mill-sawn board kerf marks were even, straight and vertical.

The Steam-Driven Circular Saw

This saw, part of the change brought by the Industrial Revolution, made its appearance about 1820. A mechanized means of sawing logs using the rotary blade, with cutting therefore continuous, it produced a widely curving or circular kerf mark. From 1820 onwards, power-driven circular blades have been used for reducing logs to lumber and for other refinements, hence the simple but important conclusion that a piece of furniture showing circular kerf marks on its inside or secondary surfaces (surfaces which have not received final dressing) must have been constructed after the year 1820. Note these marks on the photographed Victorian desk-drawer bottom (illustration 26).

An 18th-century piece of furniture conversely should show signs of straight kerf marks. For example, straight kerf marks may be found on the back, on the inside and on the underside of a veneered walnut Queen Anne–period highboy. This evidence should remain on at least one of the above-mentioned surfaces to support authenticity, although many times surfaces were planed smooth. If there are no straight marks, or circular marks are found instead (often the ridges can be felt when they cannot be seen) the piece must be questioned; the available kerf-mark evidence certainly does not agree with the constructional detail appropriate to a piece of that period.

25. Saw kerf marks:

    a. Straight kerf marks.
    b. Curving kerf marks.

a.

b.

26. Mid-19th-century desk-drawer bottom, showing circular-saw marks.

Turner.

27. *The turner at his lathe as pictured in* The Book of
English Trades, *1807. "The thing to be turned is fixed on
the lengthened axis of the smaller wheel, and upon the prop
or rest, the chisel or other cutting instrument is supported;
and being brought to touch the wood while it is swiftly
turning round, it takes off shavings to the greatest nicety."*
Photograph courtesy the American Antiquarian Society.

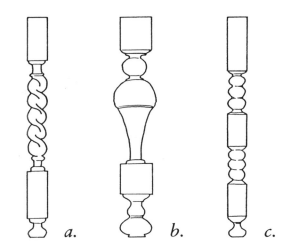

TURNING OF THE WOOD

The skill of turning (or cutting) on a lathe is a fascinating and ancient craft. (Turning is the practice of shaping objects by means of stationary cutting tools brought into contact with objects held and rotated rapidly on a lathe.) Thus, the final turned shape must be contained within the square section of wood from which it was worked. Lathes, rediscovered in 17th-century England, have been used in some capacity despite fashion changes ever since. Like the saw, lathes were gradually mechanized, until turning is an automatic operation today, but, during the 17th and 18th centuries, successful turning was literally in the hands of the "turner." Therefore, each of the turned legs and spindles of a piece of early furniture will be unique—no two turned legs will measure exactly the same, using a calliper, for although the legs were turned from "patterns," their final shape is the turner's deed. The obvious conclusion is thus that if the six "trumpet"-turned legs of a supposed 17th-century William and Mary highboy measure exactly the same in size and detail, they cannot have been turned by hand—the only possible means in the 17th and 18th centuries. A special form of turning, twist or spiral turning, so popular in the 17th century, was a combination of plain turning, carving, rasping and file work, plus scraping, and should consequently also prove inconsistent when measured.

Another application of the lathe is the formation of round table tops, for tea tables, candlestands, etc. All such table tops are roughed out on the lathe with the use of a rotating block or plug, which creates the surface impression. This surface is finished with a plane before proceeding with the rim carving.

28. Characteristic turned legs from the late 17th century:

a. twist-turned
b. trumpet-turned
c. baluster-turned

29. Callipers, circa 1750–1775. This tool was used repeatedly by the wood turner to check the diameter or thickness of stock being turned on a lathe. Photograph courtesy The Henry Francis du Pont Winterthur Museum.

PREPARING THE WOOD

Dressing Marks

The woodworker or cabinetmaker used many tools and made great efforts to ready his sawn pieces of timber for furniture construction. While examining secondary wood surfaces for hand-tool marks, one should be aware of the slight ridges and hollows made by the blade of the long jack plane and the further refinements of the smoothing plane, which in process have removed the kerf marks. These are called hand-plane or dressing marks and can be both seen and felt, indicating the extent to which

30. Eighteenth-century compass plane with a convex sole particularly useful for smoothing curved parts of furniture. Photograph courtesy The Henry Francis du Pont Winterthur Museum.

31. Back side of a high chest or highboy, showing dressing marks left on secondary surfaces.

32. Back side of a reeded sofa leg, a primary surface left incomplete (without reeding) due to little visibility.

the early cabinetmaker attempted to plane smooth his wood in areas which were not going to be seen. The primary surfaces were carefully smoothed, sanded and finished with oil, wax, shellac, varnish or paint, etc., the top and front generally receiving the cabinetmaker's greatest attention and effort. In contrast, many areas of primary surface with small visibility received relatively little attention: remote moldings, backsides of legs, concave surfaces of trumpet legs, etc. Note the backside of the pictured sofa leg (illustration 32) attributed to the renowned cabinetmaker Duncan Phyfe.

Of interest is the fact that there will usually be a pattern or rhythm to the marks (four grooves one time, four grooves in-between the next time, for example); the pattern will vary from man to man and from tool to tool, but it will be there. These marks were primarily made with planes and various scraping, abrading and paring tools well into the 1800s, when mass-production methods outmoded such handwork. Thus, furniture showing these marks is likely to have been made prior to 1800.

A test and method of demonstrating the presence of dressing marks in cases where these marks are neither apparent to the naked eye nor easily felt with the fingertips, is the straightedge test. By placing a rule (ruler) on top of a wood surface and spotting a light directly behind the rule, light will shine from the grooves and hollows, thereby dramatizing the dressing mark undulations. This test also demonstrates the natural grain differences of spring and summer tree growth—one shrinks more and thus is lower than the other.

Smoothing and Cutting Tools

The careful smoothing of primary surfaces was done with an assortment of planes, scrapers and sandpaper. A perfectly smooth, unblemished surface was always the goal, despite its impossibility. The simple fact that surfaces were being worked by hand implied human imperfections. Thus, the hand pressure applied by even the master craftsman on his tools would vary from movement to movement. Furthermore, some spots on the wood were softer or harder and required additional pressure. Too much pressure could be inadvertently applied, causing a slight hollow. These slight undulations or waves indicate to us that a surface was planed (or dressed) by hand—which was the necessary state of affairs for woodworkers in the 16th, 17th and 18th centuries.

Modern machine-made pieces *have* been known to have been hand-planed with old tools to emulate true antiques and have thus been mistaken by some as being old. Other construction detail will quickly destroy this illusion. Then too, genuine old pieces sometimes suffer the unhappy fate of being refinished by an amateur refinisher. His inadequate efforts, mistakes and in some cases "butchery" should never be mistaken for the handcraft of the early cabinetmaker.

Sandpapering was an important process in the final preparation of primary wood surfaces before a finish was applied. Sandpaper was valued and used by craftsmen in some form long before machine-coated modern cloths and papers were introduced in 1872. Prior to 1800, woodworkers and cabinetmakers used dried shark skin for smoothing wood. It had strong and long-lasting abrasive action with a great undercut, meaning it only cut in one direction. Abrasive papers and cloths were invented about 1800 and then they were made by hand, with resulting variations in the evenness of the coating.

33. *Early 19th-century Duncan Phyfe–style sofa (see leg detail, illustration 32).*

34. *Underside of 18th-century drawer, showing the rhythmic hand-planing marks and the bevelled edge for easier joining of the bottom into the side rebate.*

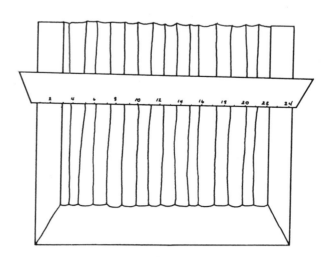

35. *Straightedge test.*

Wood: Its Characteristics and How It Is Worked · 23

36. *English mid-18th-century tea-table top with subtle reflecting surface undulations, evidence that the surface has been dressed by hand.*

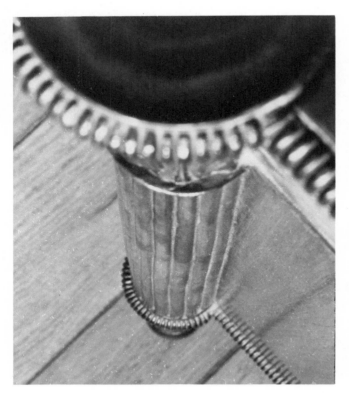

37. *Sighting down a leg to ascertain hand craftsmanship.*

Molding Planes, Gouges and Scratch Stocks

Real appreciation of undulating hand-planing marks comes when we examine the moldings made by hand with molding planes. For example, let us consider the ogee (S-shaped) molding of the panel frames belonging to a Chippendale-style secretary door. By standing as close as possible to such a molding and "sighting down" (or up), one quickly sees the unevenness of the planing. Hand-planed marks become apparent when any molding is sighted in this way—door frames, chimney moldings or the cornice moldings at the top of a secretary or highboy. Sight a modern machine-made molding and note how perfectly even it is by comparison.

This sighting test or exercise can also be used for other molded and cut surfaces to determine whether planing and cutting have been done by hand. The reeded posts of a Sheraton-style canopy bed, for example, can be sighted up and down to ascertain hand craftsmanship—hand cutting by gouges and/or a scratch stock will appear in the form of visible undulations. Note the photographed round reeded projecting leg of a Federal sideboard and the unevenness of the reeding when this detail is sighted (illustration 37). Early inlay work can also be sighted; its unevenness is due to the use of these same early hand tools.

38. *Federal sideboard of mahogany and satinwood, circa 1808–1809, Salem, Massachusetts, by William Hook. (See detail of leg, illustration 37.)*

39. *The scratch or scribe awl, with its thin round shank of iron tapering to a sharp point, was used to mark the surface of the wood with guidelines. The tool was also useful in making starting holes for the flat-ended screws in use during the 18th and early 19th centuries. This awl, 4″ long and dating between 1820 and 1850, was used in the Dominy Woodworking Shop, East Hampton, Long Island. Photograph courtesy The Henry Francis du Pont Winterthur Museum.*

Another interesting test is to take a wax impression of one section of the molding and then compare this with other sections of the molding. If the molding was really planed by hand, the impression will not match up perfectly anywhere and will vary with every inch. If the impression does match uniformly along the molding, it is reasonable to believe that it has been made by modern methods or at least machine sanded or dressed in our time.

Marking Tools

The marking tools and gauges, vital to the furniture maker in the days of total hand craftsmanship and which have since been replaced by modern, fast and perhaps more accurate methods, have left their signs on the furniture which required their use. When the important function of these tools is understood, remaining evidence of their work becomes a valuable aid in dating a piece of furniture as being very old—1830 or earlier. The awl, which resembles a modern ice pick, was used in place of today's pencil for marking all sorts of measurements needed in the construction process. The resulting scored marks or lines will be found at many points and can be quickly identified when one logically thinks through the construction process to the measurement or mark likely to have been required at that spot. For example, in examining the dovetails found on the side of a drawer, almost invariably one will find a scored gauge line (groove, mark, etc.) struck at the edge of the dovetails. This was simply the line marking the inside edge of the dovetail cutting. In the drawer photograph (illustration 46, page 34), the scored line can be seen, marking the dovetails. Measurement marks, made by a mortise gauge, can also be found near a mortise-and-tenon joint to indicate where the mortise was to be cut out.

If one studies the front legs and back uprights of old Windsor chairs and slat-back chairs made of turned parts, faint score or scribe lines can be seen. Examples can be recognized in the photograph of the child's slat-back chair (illustration 146, page 103) and on the Pilgrim chair (illustration 172, page 120). These marks were made with the blade of a chisel when the parts were turned as guides for places where holes were to be bored for cross stretchers, or where mortises were to be cut for the back slats. Such scored lines are good indications of age. Of further note is the staggering of these scored stretchers to prevent too much wood being cut from one point, a good precaution which was abandoned at a later date. Incidentally, although so many Windsor chairs were carefully stripped of their paint in the 1920s, alas the fashion then, traces of original paint can sometimes be found in the scored lines—or when a member becomes loose at its joint.

Chapter **2**

The Cabinetmaker
and Some of His
Construction Considerations

CABINETMAKER IS A HALLOWED word today. We stand in awe of his sense of design, proportion and detail and his skillful abilities to execute his plan, as we behold his product now many years old. One can quickly become absorbed in a study of individual cabinetmakers and their characteristic work. Regionalism and local schools of cabinetmakers can be explored and compared. Published books and catalogs prepared by cabinetmakers—including a 1775 Philadelphia version of Chippendale's *Director,* which was intended for production with designs by cabinetmaker John Folwell but unfortunately was never produced because of attention focused on the War of Independence—are fascinating. It should be remembered that the cabinetmaker was a simple craftsman. Some were better than others, but none imagined himself to be a great artist. Depending on how a given customer weighed the various cabinetmaking decisions—choice of wood, amount and quality of detail, kind and amount of finish, etc.—all affecting time and price—the completed piece was or was not representative of the cabinetmaker's skill. It should also be kept in mind that there are careless workers in any field and all cabinetmakers did not constantly try to do their best. It is important to keep our image of the cabinetmaker, famous or not, in proper perspective.

For the most part, woodworkers, joiners and cabinet-makers did good work and took pride in doing the best possible job within the definition of the project. At times they were most ingenious and showed a true eye for beauty, but all the while they were basically doing the job for which they had been trained by the apprentice system. In contemporary terms, they were concerned with paying the grocery bill or having the funds available for the purchase of a new vehicle. This meant that the individual craftsman moved along quickly with his projects, and hoped Mrs. Jones would pay him promptly. (If she did not he might eliminate a coat of shellac next time, especially if he was in a hurry.) How surprised, amused and pleased cabinetmakers of the 18th century, for example, would be were they to learn how they are revered today.

CHOOSING THE WOOD

Like all businessmen (Thomas Chippendale has been described as the first successful interior decorator/designer), cabinetmakers had many practical decisions to make with regard to each piece of furniture. Wood considerations, including the choice of wood, were critical. Soft woods, cheap and available, were utilized in

27

40. *Carved claw-and-ball foot, circa 1760–1780, Newport. The Townsend-Goddard families of cabinetmakers were unique in America in their abilities to open-cut the talons on their claw-and-ball feet. This superb example not only has the sides of the ball free, but it is possible to run a thread over the top of the ball.*

areas not seen and where strength was not necessary, such as drawer interiors. Costly hardwoods were used to provide strength and for their handsome appearance in parts that were seen. "Green" hardwoods were selected for turning, this wood state being relatively soft and hence making the turning task easier.

The pierced and carved splat of a Chippendale-style chair, so inherently weak by design, required a hard, strong wood to resist the pressure of a seated person's back. Bed rails and chair legs both required strong woods to do their jobs of supporting much weight. Indeed, without the popularity and ability of walnut, cherry and mahogany—all hardwoods—to support the weight of a chest of drawers (filled) on tall slender legs, the highboy could not exist. The cabinetmaker's sophisticated craftsmanship, showing his control of the strain put upon his chosen wood and its ability to withstand this pressure, can be seen in the carved claw-and-ball foot of a Townsend-Goddard mahogany high chest of drawers or highboy. So strong is the wood that the talons have been open-cut and the great weight of the piece rests on a much reduced area.

The quality of the kind of wood selected was also a consideration. Knots, for example, were an unwelcome flaw and weakness in all wood. They often would fall out and while present play havoc with any applied finish. Fortunately, it was possible to obtain wood without this imperfection and this was done whenever possible.

Cabinetmakers have always selected their woods carefully for the purposes planned. In addition to quality and strength of the chosen wood, its color and indeed the beauty and interest of the grain's figure were important. Duncan Phyfe, working in New York between 1795 and 1847, so loved and admired figured mahogany that he eliminated most ornament and detail to allow the wood to show its full glory.

Cabinetmakers and patrons alike have admired the beauty of exciting wood figure. To work up patterns for matched drawer and door fronts and to utilize the interesting figure of woods whose source is an unusual circumstance and whose future movement is unpredictable (burls and whorls) is a challenge to the veneering skill of the cabinetmaker. Veneering also conserves highly figured wood.

The cabinetmaker accomplished his goals and produced the superb products which are so loved and admired today through great understanding—indeed, scientific knowledge in part—of his basic material—wood. Some of this understanding came from trial and error experience; some came from lessons learned while serving as an apprentice or working in a joiner or cabinetmaking shop, and some came from an innate love and interest in the material. There are few crafts in which one works with a material that is in a perfectly natural state. Most substances are purified or manufactured, whereas wood comes to the plane and chisel as it grew in the forest.

WOOD MOVEMENT

The knowledge and understanding developed by the furniture maker placed him on guard for some of the problems posed by wood. Wood movement was a serious concern, in the stages of construction and after the piece of furniture was completed. Since wood shrinks and swells, seasonally and daily, due to changes in the moisture content of the atmosphere, seasoning newly cut timber was an important first step in stabilizing the moisture content of the wood. The movement would not be so great thereafter. Various finishes applied to wood surfaces also kept movement to a minimum.

Details and kinds of construction were sometimes adopted to allow for this. Panel-and-frame construction was a clever way of overcoming difficulties caused by such movement (see Chapter 4). As the panel expanded with additional moisture absorption it filled the leeway space in the grooved frame. Illustration 41 shows this kind of construction where the frame has come partly away. As the panel shrank with reduced moisture, it was free to contract away from the frame and thus not split from being held in place. Again as a reaction to wood movement, cabinetmakers occasionally extended the length of a drawer bottom beyond its frame at the back, to serve not only as a drawer stop but as assurance that extra wood would be there if needed because of bottom spaces caused by shrinkage.

The understanding of wood movement was sometimes used to advantage. The effectiveness of old cornerblocks suggests this. A very common example is the corner foot block of a bracket foot. The grain of the interior foot block is vertical, while that of the bracket-foot facings is horizontal. The tendency is for the bracket foot to shrink and become lower in winter and swell slightly in summer while the block foot remains the same height (its shrinkage is horizontal), thus performing its function of support. This movement in time causes the glue to give way, which also explains why the foot block may be missing, leaving the weight of the case to be precariously carried by the bracket facings. Another example would be the triangular horizontal-grain cornerblock found supporting the legs of a mid-18th-century Massachusetts slip-seat chair. Again, the tensions complement each other.

Many of the cabinetmaker's techniques and uses of wood depended on minimum wood movement; some-

41. *Seventeenth-century oak front chest panel of panel-and-frame construction. Note how the panel is recessed into the lower rail.*

The Cabinetmaker and Some of His Construction Considerations · 29 times this gamble was successful, and sometimes telltale signs and shrinkage problems were the result. There were times, as well, when fashion and novelty seem to have overruled wisdom in choice of construction material and method. Again it must be remembered that the furniture-maker through history has always been engaged in trade.

Many tricks of the trade learned and adopted by the furniture maker bear witness to his knowledge, sensitivity and sensibility towards his craft. Awareness of wood's tendency to split along its grain meant that the individual nails or screws in a row would be slightly staggered so as not to crack the board grain. Another device was to position the stretchers of a Windsor chair at different levels to obtain maximum support. The appropriate choice of joint for a given purpose was another important decision, and one made well most of the time judging from the number of untouched old joints still doing their intended jobs today.

There is much question as to the cabinetmaker's awareness and consideration for the effect of patina—the soft mellow surface look achieved by a combination of factors over time. The cabinetmaker may have admired the patina surface of old furniture in his time, though there is little reference or evidence of this. Certainly the cabinetmaker admired the wood with which he worked and was eager to preserve and enhance its beauty with the best possible bright finish. His longer-range concern, I think, was preservation. The subtle changes and effects we call patina today can be considered a modern pleasure and a special bonus—the result of the cabinetmaker's skill but not directly attributable to it. We were not there, however, and thus will never know for certain.

a.

b.

c.

42. *Cornerblock examples, showing strength usefulness of wood-grain direction.*

a. Open strut/cross-brace cornerblock, characteristic of England and Portsmouth, N.H.

b. Solid two-piece quarter-round cornerblock attached with glue, characteristic of Philadelphia and Connecticut.

c. One-piece bracket or triangular-shaped cornerblock attached with glue and nails or screws, characteristic of Massachusetts.

Chapter 3

Joinings

DISCOVERING HOW AND WHERE the parts of a piece of furniture are joined together has all the fascination of a jigsaw puzzle. Locating the joinings can be a real challenge, especially in cases where they have been well disguised. (French ébénistes or cabinetmakers were particularly skilled at concealing their joined areas.) The decisions as to where to join the parts of a piece were important, as the end result had not only to work well structurally and withstand stress and strain given the function of the piece, but to be aesthetically pleasing as well. (See illustration 43 to see how certain chairs, tables and chests have been joined.)

To aid the cabinetmaker with his joining task were a variety of joints he could employ, as well as hardware (nails and screws) and adhesives, i.e., glue, to reinforce his choice. Of the many joints known and used by early furniture makers, each had its own characteristics, functions and best uses. The cabinetmaker understood this well, judging from what we observe in old pieces. Not only did he use the most effective joint for a particular joining, but he worked out the correct proportions to hold the piece firmly together right up to today. He clearly took great pride in the craftsmanship necessary to make a joint which fitted together and worked

perfectly. One of the joys in exploring old joints is the sense it gives of the cabinetmaker's pride and skill. Another joy is the variety of joints and the variations on any given type that one finds when one takes the time to look closely and to understand.

JOINTS

Dovetail Joint

The dovetail joint is one of the oldest and most successful joints in furniture-making history. Whether hand- or even machine-cut, it is still the best method of joining two pieces of wood together in their width at right angles to each other. At a typical auction, showing or antique shop, one will often see people pulling out the drawers of case pieces and seemingly studying or admiring the dovetails—so-called because one part is tapered in shape rather like a dove's tail and fits into a corresponding wedge-shaped recess. By its shape it thus resists any outward pull. For a typical drawer, the part on the front is the tenon called the pin and the counterpart side

31

43. *Furniture joinings.*

mortise is called the tail. The dovetail joint is a challenge to the talents of all cabinetmakers. Handmade dovetails, with their subtle irregularities and variety of sizes can be easily spotted as such in comparison with the regular, rather short and stubby machine-made dovetails—a good first indication that the piece in question is indeed old and handmade. A scored line will also be visible, marking the gauge line of hand-cut dovetails. Further evidence of hand-cut dovetails appears on the interior front-corner areas of drawers—horizontal cuts will indicate that a dovetail saw (rather than a chisel) has been used and thus the saw has overshot the area of cutting, leaving apparent kerf marks. (Such marks can be seen in illustration 111, p. 74.)

Cabinetmakers have a traditional rule for dovetail measurements. All dovetails are made on variations of the proportions of 3″ up (in the vise) and ⅝″ across. (See illustration 45.) These proportions apply regardless of the length or the number of dovetails planned. The best angle for the dovetail is about 12 degrees. If the slope or pitch is made steeper, the corners will tend to break off; if made shallower, the dovetail will be weak.

Dovetails found on late 17th- and early 18th-century drawers tend to be large, rough and chiseled by hand; nevertheless they serve their constructional purpose very well. The dovetail became more refined during the 18th century and directly reflected the skill of the individual cabinetmaker. Country cabinetmakers tended to make

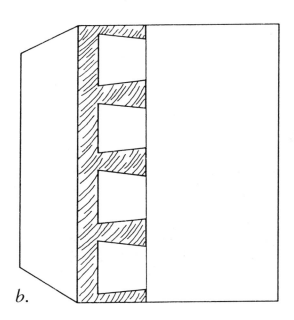

44. *Kinds of dovetails:*

a. Fine hand-cut single-lapped dovetail joining. This joint is used for drawers, etc., where one face must not show the joint and the dovetails are thus set back by a small lap. The angle or slope of the dovetail constitutes its holding power against lateral strain.

b. Hand-cut single-lapped dovetail joining. The slopes of the dovetail sides usually vary slightly since the cabinetmaker generally cuts them out freehand without using a bevel.

c. Machine-cut single-lapped dovetail joining. The pins (sometimes called keys) and tails are uniform and exactly the same size. No gauge line is necessary.

45. Traditional dovetail measurement.

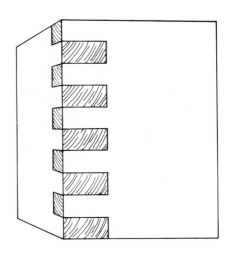

46. Hand-cut drawer dovetails. The dovetails are wider than the pins or recesses (which run almost to a point), and the dovetail slopes vary slightly one from the next. Note vertical scored line at the root of the drawer dovetails, serving as a guideline for consistent dovetail length.

48. Late 19th-century pine drawer with mechanical pin-and-scallop dovetail-type joining. The drawer side was scalloped to fit into the drawer-front matching scallops and over the drawer-front side protruding "pins" (dowels). The Knapp dovetailing machine was patented in 1877 by Charles B. Knapp and Nathan Clement, Waterloo, Wisconsin.

straightforward, husky dovetails with few in number per drawer side, thereby taking minimum risk of mishap during the cutting process. In contrast, when one finds carefully cut, geometrically correct dovetails with many per drawer side, one knows the piece to be the work of a master craftsman. Put another way, without so much as opening the drawer of a beautiful 18th-century Philadelphia dressing table, one might well expect to find very fine dovetails.

Machine-cut dovetailing, often with eight or more small dovetails per drawer side, was introduced during the nineteenth century. Machine-cut dovetails are easy to identify, being evenly spaced, symmetrical and uniform. (The pins between the dovetails will often prove the counterpart of the dovetail in size and shape.) Some late 19th-century factory furniture was held together with a pin-and-scallop joint called the Knapp joint.

There are many variations of the handmade dovetail joint. We will limit ourselves here to a brief descriptive summary for purposes of recognition, since more detailed information is available in any woodworking book or dictionary.

47. Machine-cut square through dovetail with tails and pins of equal size.

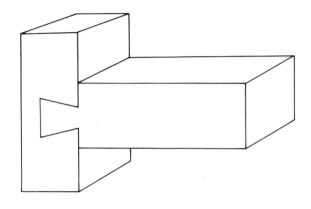

49. Secret (double lap) dovetail joint. The dovetails are set back by a small lap on both faces of the joint.

50. Slot (slide) dovetail joint. This joint can be bare-face (tapered on one face only), double-tapered (as shown) or stopped (this the most laborious as it cannot be sawn through but must be chiseled out and hence is used only where the actual joints must be hidden on one face).

The single-lapped dovetail is a joint used commonly in core, box and drawer construction, in which one part, usually with the pins, has a lap or covering piece so that the ends of the dovetails are concealed (see illustration 44). Its particular value is in core work in which the joint does not show on one face. (When veneer is anticipated for drawer parts, the lapped dovetail also eliminates possible veneer-adhering problems due to through-dovetail end grain.) The double-lapped or secret-lapped dovetail is a dovetail joint in which both joining pieces have a lap. The lap in one piece is allowed to project. Thus, the only indication of the presence of the joint is the thin line of end grain. This joint is often used for the tops of bureaux and cabinets.

Slot (slide) dovetails are cut in the width rather than the thickness of the wood and are used in plinths, cornices, etc. This is a heavy-duty joint, and illustration 51 shows how it was used to anchor the four legs into the pedestal of an Empire card table. Note how the veneer damage of the desk-and-bookcase (illustration 139, page 95) exposes a drawer support with slot dovetail joint. (This is also called a dovetail housing joint.)

The mitre dovetail (or secret mitre) is a corner joint in which the dovetail is entirely concealed. This joint is used chiefly for outside joints, plinths and work in which it is desirable to hide the joint. The Chinese considered mitring the most beautiful form of jointing parts of furniture and used the mitre dovetail and mortise-and-tenon joints extensively, along with panel-and-frame construction. In fact, the mitred dovetail was so refined by the Chinese cabinetmaker that the dovetails are completely hidden on both sides. (See the Chinese chair seat, illustration 6, page 5.)

51. Underside of pedestal base, Empire card table. The four legs are slot dovetailed into the pedestal base, and the pedestal base is joined to the pedestal in the center with a reinforced (wedged) through-tenon mortise-and-tenon joint.

52. *Mitre dovetail joint. The mitre or secret mitre dovetail.*

Mortise-and-Tenon Joint

The strongest, perhaps oldest, and most versatile of all joints is the mortise and tenon (see illustration 3). This joint is such that one piece has a projection (the tenon) which fits into a corresponding recess (the mortise) chiseled out of the other piece. Used most successfully as the major joint in chair construction, this is an important joint in table construction as well, particularly in the form of the bridle joint which joins the legs to the table. The mortise-and-tenon joint is also used for all kinds of framing. It is used for connecting the rails and headboard of a bed and for uniting the four sides of a case piece. Sometimes this joint is pegged to provide even greater strength, and these pegs will always be visible. Other variations of the mortise-and-tenon joint include the haunch tenon, the through tenon, the blind tenon and the wedge tenon. (An example of a wedge tenon can be seen in illustration 51, where it is used to anchor the pedestal to the base platform of the table.) The socket tenon joint with a rounded tenon fitting into a rounded hole, particularly suited for the joining of turned chair parts, can be considered another form of the mortise-and-tenon joint.

The draw-bore-pin joint is a form of mortise-and-tenon joint of great strength and tightness. Because of its power, this joint is used in massive-structure joinery—a bed rail for a heavy bedpost, for example. Through a special technique, the mortise-and-tenon joint is locked and the tenon is forced home into its mortise. This is done by passing a peg or pin through staggered holes in both parts of the joint, thereby exerting pressure on the joint. That is to say, a hole is bored right through the mortised piece, the tenon put in position, and the bit pressed into the hole so that it marks the tenon. The

53. *Mortise-and-tenon joint.*

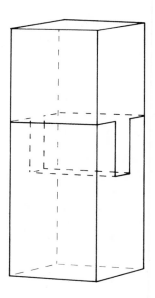

54. *The bridle joint, sometimes referred to as a "slot" mortise-and-tenon joint, is marked out with a mortise gauge, which is worked from the face sides and set to give a slot about ⅓ the total thickness, with equal wood left on either side.*

tenon is then withdrawn and its hole bored slightly nearer the shoulder. A draw-bore-pin (a tapered rod) is then knocked into the hole, forcing the two off-center holes to meet. The pin is then withdrawn and a wooden peg is inserted.

Mitre Joint

The common mitre joint has always been considered an important and useful joint by cabinetmakers and is one easily recognized by students. It is formed by the intersection of two moldings or two plain pieces of wood. The angle at which the molding is cut should halve the overall angle of the joining pieces, and since most moldings join at right-angles, the mitring angle is 45 degrees. (A simple example would be the mitred corners of a picture frame.) On occasion a curved molding joins a straight molding of the same section; thus the mitre joint must be curved. By locating and studying mitre joints, students of furniture can ascertain whether they were

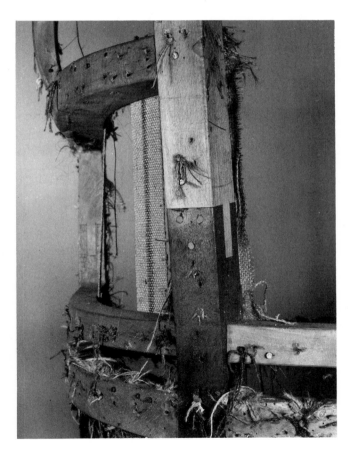

55. The bridle joint here forms a strong connection between the rear leg of the wing chair and the back frame support. (See illustration 94, page 64, for an overall photograph of this stripped barrel-back wing chair.)

56. Through-tenon mortise-and-tenon joint. The tenon extends through the chair stile for greater strength, thereby showing end grain on the rear edge of the stile. The joint is frequently found in Chippendale-style rococo Philadelphia chairs of the mid-18th century.

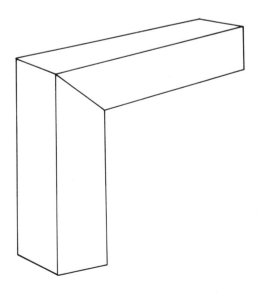

57. True mitre joint.

properly made for their time and whether or not they have been tampered with since. This is helpful for dating purposes. The same reasoning, of course, can be applied to all traditional old joints.

Rule Joint

To those with mechanical minds, the rule joint provides special appeal. It is at its most fascinating and attractive when used for its main purpose, the leaves of a drop-leaf table. (Note the rule joint on the drop-leaf table, illustration 162, page 114.) The idea of the rule joint is that where the extension leaf hangs down, the ovolo (half-round) edge is seen. This becomes invisible when the leaf is raised. The rule joint derives its name from its approximation to the brass joint of the cabinetmaker's rule and its use dates back to the early 1700s. This type of joint is still used today, there being little difference between the old and modern joints except that in some of the old ones the curved lip of the joint is noticeably less than half the thickness of the table top. Unfortunately, however, this joint is inherently weak. It cracks easily and is difficult to repair, especially when the trouble is combined with hinge problems.

Knuckle Joint

The knuckle joint is related to the rule joint in design and purpose. Swing legs for card and occasional tables are hinged to the underframing of the table with this type of joining.

Dowelled Joint

One of the less skillful means of joining two pieces of wood is with wooden dowels. A dowel is a round wooden peg, and any form of joint in which dowels are used to hold parts together is called a dowelled joint. The machine-made dowel is glued into holes bored by machine into the two pieces to be joined. Dowels in a variety of materials have been used for a variety of purposes since ancient times, but dowelled joints tend to appear in less important late 19th- and early 20th-century work to replace the mortise and tenon. Dowelled joints provide a cheap and quick method of joinery but are comparatively weak, the rounded peg providing the minimum adhesion surface for glue, so that any strain on the joint or shrinkage in the surrounding wood is likely to cause the joint to fail. Examples of 18th-century furniture with dowelled joints are unknown. (This joint should not be confused with the pegged joint, in which a wooden pin is passed through a mortise and tenon to hold the two firmly together.)

58. Rule joint.

59. Knuckle joint.

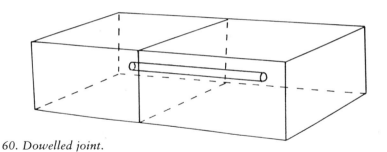

60. *Dowelled joint.*

PEGS

Pegs alone have been used in some form from the beginning of furniture making and continue to be an important construction material today. Used to fasten parts together, wooden pegs (or pins) were easy to make—in whatever size or shape needed to do the job—and they were much cheaper than nails. Early glues were not as reliable in terms of holding power, with their content varying tremendously, so that upon scrutiny of 17th-century furniture, one finds only hand-cut wooden pegs holding the boards together.

Pegs were chiseled from stringy, sinewy, elastic hardwoods such as oak, ash and beech. They were never perfectly round and occasionally they were tapered. Although driven tightly into round holes, in time they would work their way out, partially due to the shrinkage of the surrounding wood and partially due to the relatively slight shrinkage of the peg itself. (Notice the extended pegs in the old joint stool, illustration 217, page 152.) Sometimes a hump (bow) was carved right into the peg. Consequently, when the humped peg was inserted and forced to straighten, the extra pressure from the forced hump would help the peg cling to the mortise and tenon. The humped peg was, in fact, acting like a spring joint.

Some case pieces are made with pegs alone. Pilgrim chairs, tables and chests were primarily constructed with pegs, as were the Pilgrim houses. The Windsor chair, too, is constructed with wedged pegs and without the aid of glue.

ADHESIVES

Cabinetmakers have also made use of "glue" in the construction of furniture. More properly defined as an adhesive, a substance used for joining or bonding other materials together by surface attachment, glue has been used since prehistoric times. As of the 17th century, with the veneering of furniture and use of applied moldings, bosses and split spindles for decoration, plus wood blocks in general, effective glue was essential. Many joints were reinforced with glue. These first adhesives were probably natural gums and waxes such as resin, rubber, shellac and beeswax, all of which are exuded by certain insects and trees and still find limited use. Very early, the ancient Egyptians employed animal glues in making wood furniture and attaching ornamental veneers to wood surfaces.

The three principal adhesive types are animal and fish ("hide glue"), vegetable (modern rubber latex and extrine) and the synthetics, so called "white glues." Animal and fish glues are made from hides and bones and are, in fact, an impure form of gelatin. Traditionally (and out of necessity until 35 years ago, when a cold liquid hide glue was perfected) animal glue is applied hot and hardens both by cooling and by the absorption or evaporation of water. When evidence of glue is found on furniture up through the 19th century, it will necessarily be a form of hide glue, as this was the only kind available.

If furniture appears to have been glued with white glue, this is evidence that the piece has been recently reglued, that it is not very old or that it may be false, requiring further scrutiny. This is because synthetic adhesives were not developed until the 1930s. White glue is by far the strongest of the adhesives used by modern cabinetmakers, is relatively fast-working and does not deteriorate. Indeed, white glue is so effective that once used on old furniture for repairs, should the damage reoccur, it will be almost impossible to reverse early white-glue work to make new repairs. Generally speaking, soluble hide glue should be used for all glue work on old furniture; however, the use of white glue for restoration of clean breaks where strength is important may be the preference.

SHOE PIECES

Techniques of joining are the very essence of old-furniture construction, and its study is never-ending. Once one has a comfortable understanding of the basic joints, for example, one can identify and muse on the varieties of shoe piece found at the base of the splat, in fact supporting the splat on mid-18th-century side and open armchairs. This important member served its function as a separate piece into which the splat was usually mortised at the top, after which the shoe piece was attached to the top of the back seat rail. With some chairs the shoe is really two separate pieces, supporting the splat on each side. Occasionally one finds the shoe supporting the splat at its base from behind. Whichever version is used, the shoe will usually be there as a separate and necessary part of 18th-century-period chairs (18th-century Southern American chairs tend not to have separate shoes). Later 18th-century-style chairs usually incorporate the shoe function into the back seat rail as one piece of wood, primarily for reasons of expediency.

61. Chair shoe pieces.

62. Chair back shoe piece as found on most mid-18th-century side chairs. In this example the splat is mortised into this one-piece shoe member which in turn is attached (often nailed) to the top of the back seat rail.

63. *Seventeenth-century oak "hung" drawer with lap-jointed nailed corners.*

DRAWER JOININGS

An appropriate conclusion to a discussion about joinings would be a comparison of joined drawers which, by their joining, aid in the dating of a case piece. Starting with the early 17th-century drawer, illustration 63 and 64 show that this drawer is simply lap-jointed at the corners and then nailed to reinforce the joint. (This drawer is also described as a "hung" drawer because it moves along on a runner extending from the case interior which fits into the groove cut into the drawer side; hence, the drawer "hangs.") The boards of the bottom, running front to back, were nailed into a rebate in the lower side of the front.

In the late 17th century, the practice of strengthening drawer joints with nails was replaced by the stronger dovetail joint. The introduction of walnut-veneered furniture came at this time and the drawer linings became thinner. This lighter construction was made possible by dispensing with the runner grooves in the drawer sides; this newer drawer slid in and out of the interior on the board forming the drawer bottom. The bottom of the drawer still had the wood grain running from front to back.

With the change to mahogany, mid-18th century, further drawer-construction changes evolved. The single-lapped dovetail joinings became narrower and more numerous. Improvement in the bottom wearing surface consisted of fitting additional pieces of wood, called runners, to the bottom inside edges of the drawer sides to withstand the friction of wear caused by use. The grain of the bottom then ran side to side, and properly fitted it was glued into the groove in the front and free to swell and shrink at the back. This drawer, often with a lip-molded front of solid mahogany, i.e., the drawer front projecting beyond the core to which it was fitted (see illustration 221, page 155), was made until about 1750, when veneered fronts of mahogany became more common and cock-bead moldings were applied (rabbeted joining) to the edges of the drawer fronts. This type of drawer is shown on an English secretary (illustration 148, page 104) and on a chest of drawers (illustration 8, page 11).

A further central joining was sometimes used in the drawer bottom when the drawer was particularly wide. By inserting a muntin through the center of the drawer bottom (see illustration 68), smaller, thinner boards could be used and maximum strength was obtained. At the end of the 18th century and into the 19th century, particularly in England, quarter-round moldings were glued into the interior drawer edges. Again, this served as a form of strength for the joints, but also it eliminated the possibility of dust and grit collecting in the corners.

64. Seventeenth-century "hung" drawer. Note thick sides to accommodate runner grooves and bottom wood-grain direction running from front to back.

65. Late 17th-century English and early 18th-century American walnut-veneered drawer front with thinner drawer linings and dovetail joining.

66. Lip-molded solid mahogany drawer front, circa 1740 in England and 1760–1785 in America. Note fine lapped dovetail joinings and side-to-side grain direction. The bottom is contained in a groove in front and in rebates in the sides, with runners beneath to widen the bearing surfaces and to prevent the bottom from scraping. The back stands above the bottom.

67. Applied cock-bead molding mahogany-veneered drawer front, its appearance in England beginning with early 18th-century walnut furniture and continuing through the 18th century. Its American use dates to the late 18th century and continues into the 19th century. The moldings fit at the sides into rebates in the drawer front, the lap of the dovetails being made wide enough to give a reasonable seating for them.

68. Characteristically English late 18th-century or early 19th-century drawer with muntin partition or cross-bar.

Chapter **4**

Panelling and Moldings

PANELLING

THE RECTANGULAR PANEL-WITHIN-A-FRAME form for chest construction appeared in the late 15th century and was generally used for both furniture and architecture in the 16th century. This was joinery in the truest sense: panel-and-frame construction put together with mortise-and-tenon joints by the woodworker, now called a joiner. Such construction (see illustration 69) insured that the object would be relatively limited in material, i.e., prior to use of this method, the chest had been composed totally of solid, thick and thus heavy boards. Panel-and-frame construction required the strength of solid rails and stiles (the horizontal and vertical framing members) with average measurements 2½″ to 3″ wide and 1″ to 1½″ thick. The inner edge grooves of the rails and stiles held the much thinner (and thus lighter) central panels, ⅜″ to ¾″ thickness in the middle, tapering to a 3/16″ tongue at the edges. Lightness represented an economy of material but, more importantly, made for easier handling of the final product without loss of strength or utility. In fact, this method allowed for greater flexibility and variety in the use of wood. Suddenly the walls of rooms could be panelled in wood, sometimes 20′ high, and thus made warmer in winter. The enormous, magnificent Elizabethan beds of the 16th century could never have been created without the relative lightness and resiliency of this form of construction.

The rectangular framing of thin panels had the unique advantage of minimizing the natural acts of warping, splitting, twisting and shrinking, because the panel rested loosely in its grooves in the upright stiles and horizontal rails. Hence it was free to move, to expand and contract with humidity and temperature changes, and to "give" if need be. This elasticity was a deterrent to various forms of bursting. When a panel was not left free to move but was held at the edge(s) and thus could not react to atmospheric conditions, shrinkage cracks and other damage appeared. Notice the left panel in the late 17th-century chest (illustration 71). The panel has been held fixed—perhaps the wood swelled tightly into the groove or perhaps dirt and wax filled the groove space so as to secure the panel firmly. Whatever the reason, when shrinkage movement took place, the panel could not move and a crack was the result. Consider as well the example of the desk-and-bookcase door panel (illustration 152, page 108). Shrinkage has moved the panel

44

69. Panel-and-frame construction as here represented with linen-fold-pattern carved panels set into the pegged mortise-and-tenon-joined frame of an oak 16th-century chest. Note in the vertical section detail how the panel rests loosely in its frame, thereby having freedom to expand and contract with atmospheric temperature and humidity changes.

70. An Elizabethan bed of the late 16th century with panelled headboard and tester.

71. Seventeenth-century American oak and pine chest, panel-and-frame construction with shrinkage crack in front panel.

Panelling and Moldings · 45

72. *Cross-grain walnut applied cornice moldings characteristic of the 1695 William and Mary style. The flat surfaces and large curved surfaces, such as this center ovolo molding section, were veneered; the rest was built up with cross-grained walnut, usually on a softwood groundwork.*

partially out of its grooved frame. No harm has come to the panel with this method of construction, but, unfortunately, the cabinetmaker has underestimated the possible panel movement in planning the width of his serpentine-shaped upright side stile. Another example of this flexible construction is the raised field panel in the painted Swedish cupboard door (illustration 128, page 84), which has moved without mishap for over 200 years.

Panel-and-frame construction using mortise-and-tenon joinery declined in use with the introduction of veneer work in the late 17th century. (Where veneer was not intended—for example on tables, chairs and stools—panel-and-frame construction was used.) When a flat surface was necessary, however, to receive veneer, the uneven panel-and-frame surface was not appropriate. Smooth, flat core-stock surfaces for adhering walnut and mahogany veneers were constructed by building up the cores from oak or pine boards glued side by side; these were trimmed to shape and joined along the abutting edges of sides, top and bottom with rows of dovetails set in glue. The exploded chest of drawers shown in illustration 43, page 32, describes this jointing procedure beneath the veneer. Due to broken and missing veneer of the lower section of a desk-and-bookcase (illustration 139, page 95), one can see where the drawer rail has been dovetail jointed into the abutting side of the case, thereby maintaining the flat surface of the core to receive the flat underside of the veneer. Panel-and-frame construction was still used for parts where possible—cabinet and cupboard doors, for example, were worked in solid wood. An understanding of this form of construction, along with the different kinds of moldings and their methods of construction, is very helpful in dating a piece of furniture.

MOLDINGS

Moldings, scratched in crudely or achieved with the use of a molding plane or scratch stock (both having irons cut to the desired profile) often decorated the edges of the framing (the stiles and rails) around panels. An example of such decoration can be seen in illustration 71. Hence, moldings true to their architectural function of providing decorative treatment enliven plain surfaces with their play of light and shade and accent the lines and design of the furniture.

Moldings in the 17th century were worked in the solid, i.e., the framing edge was being molded. Such a molding moves inward from the surface. Again note illustration 71. During the 17th century it also became customary to decorate furniture with applied moldings (and ornaments such as bosses and split spindles) glued and bradded into position. These moldings projected beyond the surface of the piece, being applied to the structure. The New England 17th-century press cupboard drawer shown in illustration 63, page 41, is a dramatic example of this.

Curved moldings at this time were sometimes cut with carving tools, making the surface appreciably irregular;

73. *Straight-grain solid molding of mahogany with a backing of softwood.*

at other times the scratch stock was used, resulting in greater molding-surface irregularity. Some applied curved moldings in the late 17th century were large circular arches, and these were turned on a lathe, like a gigantic pair of split spindles. Domed hoods of clock cases and writing cabinet friezes were areas where these large ovolo moldings were frequently applied. Regardless of the tool used and the effect desired, moldings were the result of hand work and hand pressure. Consequently, slight variations can be felt as one passes one's finger along a molding, and these same undulations can be observed if one sights down or along these moldings.

The applied molding reached its height in the 18th century. Such moldings were constructed in a variety of ways. In the Walnut Period, moldings were invariably cross-grained—as with a cross-grained, half-round walnut cornice molding on a William and Mary–style highboy. From the time of mahogany, followed by satinwood, cornice moldings were usually straight-grained and were applied in two forms: (1) with a backing of soft wood, and (2) as a built up composite of several pieces of wood.

Many moldings were carved before being applied. This carving emphasized the characteristic details of the fashion in furniture at the time. Sometimes cornice moldings were carved with egg-and-dart detail or acanthus leafage. (Note the carved, gilded molding surrounding the secretary panel in illustration 152, page 108). The rococo moldings, sometimes called "streamer" moldings, applied with glue and nails to Philadelphia Chippendale-style highboys and lowboys, are superb and repeat the S and C curves of the cabriole legs and curving pediments.

Another enrichment to the molding was the applied fret, or superimposed pierced wood tracery, which often serves like an applied carved type of molding, for instance on case pieces as friezes. Then, too, sometimes the fret surface has been carved. Along with the fret, completely cut out before application, is the dentil molding, which is executed in a similar way and is usually added under a built-up (composite) cornice. (See illustration 74.)

The cock-bead molding, added frequently to accent drawer-front edges and to protect drawer-front veneers, was another handsome form of molding. An example of

74. *Composite molding built up of several pieces of wood. Note the applied dentil molding and the applied fret. This type of molding is associated with large moldings.*

75. Applied rococo moldings on a 1760–1770 Philadelphia mahogany dressing table of outstanding craftsmanship. Photograph courtesy the Museum of Fine Arts, Boston.

76. Corner of scallop-edged mahogany tea table, Boston, circa 1750, with cracked tray top.

this can be seen in the dressing table in illustration 75, as well as the desk-and-bookcase drawers in illustration 148, page 104. This half-round continuous convex molding was a style characteristic and thus becomes a helpful dating consideration.

All these types of strikingly executed applied moldings made unique forms of furniture decoration possible, and many of the moldings endeavored to suggest completeness with the piece. There were, in fact, solid moldings during the 18th century, as illustrated in the tea-table detail here. The crack clearly shows the molded rim to be a continuous part of the table top. So-called pie-crust tea tables (see illustration 36, page 24) also have a solid carved rim molding, the center surface of the table having been dished out and planed smooth.

The delicate moldings in the American Federal period were occasionally inlaid with contrasting woods, in keeping with the refined use of geometric veneers and inlays characteristic of this neoclassic style. Notice such moldings on the neoclassic satinwood knife box, illustration 9, page 11.

The small, semicircular raised center astragal molding of solid wood is again the product of the molding plane; occasionally it was hand carved. It was frequently applied to glazing bars of bookcases and cabinet glass doors in the late 18th century. Using glass in doors was a special feature during this period, hence decorative molding both caught the eye and served the function of supporting the glass in place. A refined example of an astragal molding appears in the photograph of the breakfront desk-and-bookcase, illustration 126, page 82.

Finally, there is the tapered continuous-bead molding found on Hepplewhite-style square tapering legs and on the tapered sabre legs of Regency-style chairs and tripod table bases. The leg is wider at the top and the molding appears to become increasingly narrow as the leg tapers to the floor. To achieve this graduation of spacing, the scratch stock was used with the same cutter on each side to confine the tapering to the center raised area. That is to say, the beaded edges are the same width all along the edges and all gradation takes place in the center of the member.

77. Scallop-edged tea table with detailed corner. The table top is anchored to the table frame on all four sides, causing center shrinkage strain.

78. Hepplewhite-style chair and chair leg showing apparently tapered molding.

Panelling and Moldings · 49

Chapter 5

Curved Forms

79. Swan-neck finials maximizing the curved shape. Photograph courtesy the Museum of Fine Arts, Boston.

THE DEFINITION OF A CURVE is a continuously bending line without angles. This rounded flowing line in a piece of furniture attracts and leads the eye, and it is little wonder that the use of curving forms is frequently adopted by cabinetmakers. Consider, for example, the beauty of the long, delicately restrained, curving necks of the swan-neck finials on both sides of the early 19th-century American Empire–style parlor easel shown in illustrations 79 and 80.

Almost any furniture part can be curved in form: chair legs, arms, scrolled feet, ogee bracket feet, sweeping broken-scroll pediment bonnet tops to highboys, and certain moldings—ogee, ovolo, etc. It should also be noted that the curve possesses infinite variety and degree. Well known to furniture scholars is Hogarth's "line of beauty" analysis in which the celebrated painter and engraver, William Hogarth (1697–1764), evaluated a series of proportions for the cyma curve, a continuous double curve, one part being convex and the other part concave. He concluded in his 1753 book, *Analysis of Beauty*, that only one precise configuration of "waving line" should be deemed *the* line of beauty. He visually supports his conclusion with a comparison of waving lines, the Line of Beauty and Grace being No. 4, and he applies the Line to all subjects, including chair legs, corset stays and baluster-turned candlesticks.

The cabinetmaker had several alternative ways to produce a curved form, depending on the function of the furniture part involved. The swan-neck finials here presented have been carved into their curving shape and then applied to the easel frame. (Note as well the delicately carved feathers.) The scrolled, curving Flemish foot found on a Carolean-style chair or stool also represents careful planning and execution by the carver. (Such a foot can be seen on the stool in illustration 219, page 154.) The continuous cyma and reverse-cyma curves that make up the serpentine, or "French edge," found on mid-18th-century round tea tables, for instance, are further examples of carved curved ornamentation. Enjoy the silhouette of this forceful curving edge on the table top in illustration 179, page 125.

The curving shape is often incorporated in the structural parts of a piece of furniture. Many examples of successful accomplishment remain as our heritage today, and one marvels at the capabilities of cabinetmakers of the past. The cabriole leg, so-called from the French word *capriole*, meaning a caper or leap (derived from a dressage movement during which a horse leaves the ground with his forelegs tucked under and his hind legs extended in a horizontal position), is a leg curving in two directions and involving both cyma and reverse-cyma curves (see illustration 220, page 154). The challenge of execution of this leg was enormous: the planning of the wood requirement, the overall curving design and the carving

80. *Mahogany parlor easel made in New York or Boston circa 1805–1825 (see detail of finials, illustration 79).*

were all products of the master cabinetmaker's skill. The restrained classical curve of a sabre leg of a chair in the Regency or Empire style, so fashionable in the early 19th century, suggests these same master-craftsman concerns and abilities.

The bombé case pieces (case form with swelling towards the base) made in 17th-century Holland and uniquely in 18th-century Massachusetts (especially the Boston and Salem area) employed the curving shape as the major outline. Again, such pieces demanded complicated planning and execution on the part of the cabinet-maker. Critical to creating a pleasing piece of bombé furniture was the design of the curve; unless the curve

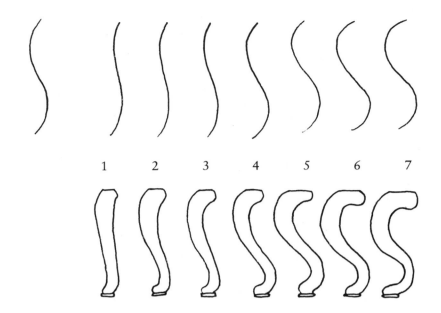

1 2 3 4 5 6 7

81. *William Hogarth's "line of beauty" analysis. Note No. 4, deemed the line of beauty.*

82. *Four-drawer chest of drawers of bombé form, probably by John Cogswell of Boston, circa 1770–1790. The drawer fronts are made of crotch-figure mahogany veneered on straight-grained mahogany. Photograph courtesy the Museum of Fine Arts, Boston.*

begins to swell outwards near the top of the second drawer, the proportions will be unsuccessful. Also of interest, as you consider the illustrations of a bombé chest of drawers shown here (illustrations 82 and 83), is that to achieve the swelling curved sides requires a costly thickness of mahogany adequate to include the fullness of the curve, which then must be carved away to create this movement. In turn the drawer fronts involve similar work, as case front and sides swell outward in counterpart directions.

The ogee bracket foot (illustration 88, page 57), is a bracket foot whose outline suggests the ogee classical molding—a double curve, convex above and concave below. Again, the cabinetmaker has carved this curving structural form from solid wood, and he has succeeded in adopting the flowing beauty of the curving line for the functional furniture part, thus creating a graceful but sturdy foot—one of the most handsome in furniture history.

No consideration of curved structural forms would be complete without considering the many curves found in chair backs and the dramatic and graceful effects they create. The serpentine curved crest rail of a Chippendale-style chair, the delicately sweeping curves of a shield-shaped back of a late 18th-century Federal chair, and the contoured high-back curves of a mid-19th-century Grecian rocker all recall the maker's skills. Many times these included the art of compound curvature, i.e., the carving out of shapes which curve in both front and side elevation, or in elevation and plan. Again the cabriole leg

83. *Bombé form, with side and front swelling outlines. Note how the drawer sides also conform to the swell of the case.*

84. *Ogee bracket foot. The curved scroll on the inside of this foot is a characteristic 18th-century Newport Townsend-Goddard cabinet-making motif.*

85. *Drawer core curvature created in brick-laying fashion.*

comes to mind, as do the early 18th-century chair backs, some of which were shaped in front elevation, side elevation and also plan (Queen Anne–style chairs, for instance). The cabinetmaker and/or carver needed to make these curves satisfactory from several directions.

To carve curved forms from solid wood is certainly an extravagant use of fine wood in that the curves require large thick boards to meet the required thickness for the curve. This in turn produces much wasted wood when it is cut away to produce the curve. The technique of veneer served in part as an alternative method for producing such pieces as bow-front and serpentine-front chests of drawers and commodes and, by the late 18th century, this method was frequently used. The technique was one of building up the desired curvature of the core stock with a series of small blocks of wood, gluing them together, sawing to shape, and then applying veneer to the exterior surface. Illustration 85 of a bow-fronted chest of drawers demonstrates this method. The entire curving front is

86. *Windsor armchair with back and arms all one continuous curving piece.*

made up of small pieces, with the vertical joints overlapping for maximum strength. In addition to little wood being used and wasted, the grain direction of the individual bricks follows the curve, thereby exposing a minimum of end grain on the surface. (Exposed end grain does not absorb glue or stain well or evenly, which leads to veneer-adhering problems.)

A variation of this technique, sometimes called coopering, is a vertical application for curving doors of hanging corner cupboards and for the curving doors of Louis XV French commodes, for example. Long, narrow strips are jointed together on a working cradle into the desired curving shape. Clamping boards at the top and bottom of the door hold the long boards in place, thereby minimizing future movement and warping. These developed surfaces are finally covered with decorative veneer.

Examples suggesting these techniques are the bow-front mahogany veneered chest of drawers (illustration 8, page 11) and the satinwood veneered knife box (illustration 9, page 11) with its curving front projection. Application of the coopering technique, working horizontally, can be recognized in the curving delicate veneered cylinder fall found on French Directoire-style cylinder writing tables or bureaux of the late 18th century.

Sometimes the "brick building" technique is passed over for the straightforward approach of carving the curved parts in the solid, and carefully applying them to the finished surface of the piece with no intention of veneer. A superb example of this would be handsomely carved and proportioned convex blocks and scallop shells applied to the case pieces made by the Townsend-Goddard cabinetmakers. The Edmund Townsend bureau table (illustration 229, page 163) has applied shells and blocks, as does the historic John Goddard desk-and-bookcase (illustration 120, page 78). Turned split spindles applied to 17th-century cupboards with glue and nails are also examples of solid curving form decoration applied to the surface of the piece.

After these difficult and sophisticated techniques for incorporating curved forms into and onto furniture, let us appreciate two very straightforward and effective methods. The first is simply cutting out the outline of the desired curve from flat wood or boards with a fretsaw. The resulting flat wood silhouette is then applied or included as part of the piece of furniture. The Chippendale-style looking glass with its elaborate scrolling apron and cresting is a good example of cut-out flat wood. (Note the outline of the looking glass, illustration 241, page 171.) Thicker wood serving a structural purpose, but cut in the same way, is exemplified in the curving scrolling foot of the late 19th-century table (illustration 125, page 81).

87. *The 1859 Thonet Nr. 14 chair consists of six parts—a long beechwood rod bent into a loop to form the back legs and chair back, a smaller loop to fit inside this and give extra support to the back, a hoop to form the framework for a caned seat, a smaller hoop to go below as a stretcher, and two tapering bent rods for the front legs. It was cheap to make, light, and transportable in parts to be assembled anywhere with fewer than ten screws—joints have been entirely eliminated.*

The curving shape of the broken-scroll pediment "bonnet top" highboy is again the product of cutting flat wood by saw. The outline shape of the scrollboard, seen from the front, derives from one large piece of cut wood. The curved solid shaped hood, called the bonnet, follows the shape of the front scrollboard and extends the depth of the piece. Construction is the result of small flat pieces of wood being cut and jointed together and glued at right angles to the scrollboard but following the curve of its outline. This delicate structure is sometimes supported by a cover of canvas glued over it. (See the broken-pediment examples in illustration 31, page 22, and illustration 228, page 162.)

A second simple and direct method for producing curved forms is the technique of bending wood. The bent or curved permanent shape is caused by subjecting the wood to heat or moisture under pressure. The bowed back of a Windsor chair represents one of the earliest forms of such bending. Hickory, oak, ash (or yew in England) with their pliable quality were used for this purpose, often in green state. The members (hoop backs and spur stretchers) were first planed to the necessary size and section and then steamed or soaked in water until

bendable. Each was then clamped in a form made of wood or metal of required shape and allowed to dry. When dry, the member retained its curvature. Some of the delicate galleried 18th-century tea tables of serpentine shape have the gallery rail bent into the conforming serpentine shape of the table top (see illustration 91, page 61).

Michael Thonet (1796–1871) perfected and developed the bentwood technique into an entire style of furniture. Beechwood was used for the Thonet process because it was resilient and had long fibers and few knots. The trunks were mechanically sawn into strips about 1″ square and then turned on a lathe, becoming circular in section. Placement in autoclaves for steaming rendered them pliable and then they were bent within metal forms and so kept until completely dry. Final shaping and finishing made the individual curved or bent parts ready for "mass production" assembly and sales distribution. Awareness of the machine with its vast capabilities and speed brought many new ideas and techniques to the furniture maker. Harnessing machinery for such uses as creating curving forms led to highly original and experimental furniture by the mid-19th century.

Curved Forms · 55

Chapter 6

Carving and Fretwork

CARVING

THE CARVING OF WOOD by hand—using special tools (chisels, gouges, files, saws and smoothing instruments) to cut three-dimensional forms out of solid wood—dates back to antiquity and has served utilitarian and decorative purposes ever since. The rich life-size carved fruit and flowers on large chests and cupboards of Renaissance Italy come immediately to mind as exuberant examples of the carver's abilities. The variety in subject, detail and scale is endless, as is the pleasure in exploring any one example for the foibles of hand craftsmanship and the ingenuity and control of the skilled carver. Feast your eyes on the superb carving on the chamfered ogee bracket foot reputedly by Samuel McIntire of Salem, Massachusetts, executed on a late 18th-century chest-on-chest. The low-relief acanthus leaves are delicately but carefully rendered with a variety of carving techniques, such as incising, undercutting, veining, fluting and shadow-carving. These are set off by the star-punched background, a kind of carving McIntire favored, judging from the frequency with which it is found on the known examples of his work.

The mid-18th century was a peak era for carving as the major form of furniture decoration. The carving of the Renaissance had set the standard and served as inspiration from then on. The 18th century drew extensively from this in its adaptation and rococo interpretations. Again in the mid-19th century, high-relief elaborate carving was revived for furniture ornamentation.

A great impetus for extensive carving during the 1740s, 1750s and 1760s was the discovery and adoption of mahogany. This beautiful rich wood was not only extremely strong, thereby allowing the Chippendale style to evolve with its delicate legs and precarious parts, but it could be successfully carved. Eighteenth-century carvers revelled in scrolled acanthus leafwork, nullings, masks, cabochons, shells and interlacing scrolls and straps. Later, less robust neoclassic carving included classical subjects, vases, festoons, drapery swags and wheat husks, along with reeding and fluting.

Low Versus High Relief

By their innate nature, carved details are an integral part of the solid wood from which they have been carved. When the joiner-carver was concerned with low-relief carving, an example of which is found on the 17th-century panelled chest (illustration 71, page 45), his

56

88. Chamfered ogee bracket foot. Photograph courtesy the Museum of Fine Arts, Boston.

wood thickness requirement was little altered since the shallow carving, chip carving, and incised lines did not penetrate deeply. He could even change his patterns and carving plans after the chest was joined because the carving was flat and flush with the surface of the piece and its depth was shallow and uniform regardless of chosen pattern. Precise symmetrical geometric patterns were achieved often with the use of a compass, and many times it is possible to find the surviving point of that compass at the center of a curvature, such as a roundel, and also remaining scribe and score lines.

Carving in greater relief demanded extensive pre-planning in the choice of wood for the specific carved detail and for the part of furniture for which it was intended. The Tudor linenfold panel, for example, molded and carved to represent a piece of folded linen, required thickness in the center and thinness at the edges to enable the panel to fit into the grooves of the framing. (See the panel thickness drawing, illustration 69, page 45.)

The cabriole leg with knee carving was a great challenge for any furniture carver, past or present. To start with, it is awkward to work out the shape on paper—i.e., since the leg is seen from several sides, including from above, it is impossible to draw on paper all the angles for which to plan. Therefore, templates or patterns of thin wood were used to mark out the curves on adjacent faces on the square block of wood. (A template enabled many legs to be marked out alike and thus matched.) As the carving progressed and the rounded leg began to emerge from the original rectangular shape, the guiding lines on the wood were cut away using frame saw and spokeshave. Everything is curved in both directions. The project became even more complicated when carving was to appear on the knee, because additional thickness of stock had to be planned. The presence of these plain blocks could distract the carver, giving a false impression of the shape as a whole. It is thus little wonder that beautifully shaped cabriole legs are rare to find and see.

The recognition of wood requirements for additional decorative carving alerts one against shallow carving of later date—often undertaken to add to the interest and value of the piece. This is called "carving up." Often,

Carving and Fretwork · 57

plain cabriole legs have carved details added to the knees. This carving will always seem surprisingly shallow in proportion to the leg, because no extra wood has been left at the knee to allow for the carving to project attractively from the main curve of the leg. An example of this can be seen in illustration 222, page 156.

Shell Carving

Carving takes many forms. Different techniques produce a variety of effects. Much depends on the goal—which becomes a cabinetmaking decision and choice. Carved convex and concave shells were often the focus of design and attention on block-front case furniture by the Townsend-Goddard families during the 1760s. (See the Edmund Townsend kneehole desk, illustration 229, page 163, and the detailed convex shell on the fall front of the desk-and-bookcase, illustration 120, page 78, attributed to John Goddard.) Many of these shells along with the blocking were carved from one solid piece of wood. Other blocks and shells were carved and then applied. (Both the desk and the desk-and-bookcase mentioned above have applied shells and blocks.) One way to determine the presence of applied work is to follow the wood grain—if it is continuous, only one piece of wood is involved. Another way is to look for join lines.

Reeding and Fluting

Reeding (or carved ribbing made up of half-round "reeds" grouped side by side) and fluting (parallel vertical grooves separated slightly by an edge in between which derives from the classical column) are types of carving that by their use of repetition brought emphasis and detail to chair legs, bedposts and pilasters on the sides of case pieces. Fluting was always cut out of the surface of the wood, using gouges. Reeding was usually cut into the wood with a scratch stock.

Finials and Pendants

Carved finials (eagles, flames, urns, etc.) found on highboys, chest-on-chests and tall clocks stand as three-dimensional sculptures in their own right. Consider the elegant cartouche so often identified with the Connecticut cabinetmaker Eliphalet Chapin, working between 1771 and 1795. Pendants, the smaller carved ornaments that point downward and are usually found attached to the lower edges of the skirts of lowboys and highboys, represent further examples of this form of carving.

Finials and pendants were carved separately and then attached with glue. Since glue unfortunately can lose its power with time, this type of attached ornamental work has, in many cases, fallen out and been lost. Often finials have not even been glued into position but fitted loosely into their socket tenons for easy, safe removal should the piece be moved. It is thus not surprising to discover foreign finials on old pieces (where someone has exercised "make do" with what they had), no finials at all, or sometimes new replacement finials. Finials and pendants should always be carefully examined to determine their relationship to the rest of the piece.

Carving with Gesso

This is one kind of carving in which the details are only roughly chiseled out in the wood. No attempt at finishing refinement is made, because the entire piece is coated with layers of whiting, called gesso, to a thickness of about ¼". When the whiting dries, the carver wets the gesso with a brush and finishes his designs by carving highlights into the gesso surface. The entire piece is then gilded or painted. Note the damaged hand rest of a French gilded chair (illustration 134, page 90) showing the layers of wood, gesso and gold leaf. This treatment has also been used for the frames of many 18th-century looking glasses. One often suspects gesso-work to have been the original treatment when one comes across a piece of furniture of fine proportions and cabinetwork but remarkably poor carving. *Has* the piece been stripped of its original gesso-carved refinement?

Pierced Carving

Sometimes carving not only decorates the surface of the wood but the carving (or cutting) is taken right through the wood for even greater decorative effect. This is called piercing or pierced carving and many examples of this technique can be cited. See, for example, the Carolean chair back (illustration 150, page 105) which incorporates piercing to emphasize the circular lines of the leafage and scrolls. Some pediments atop highboys produce a light, lattice-like effect because of piercing, as in illustration 89. The carved and pierced chair-back splats of chairs in the Chippendale and Hepplewhite styles, with their dramatic silhouettes, represent the extent to which this technique has been taken. In fact, the strength and function of the chair becomes affected (even threatened) as a result of such elaborate working of one wooden splat back. (Note the damaged chair-splat back in illustration 176, page 123.)

89. *Decorative cartouche finial.*

Carver's Pieces

True "carver's pieces," as opposed to the categories of case pieces and seat furniture, were pieces that did not have a useful function like chairs, and hence lent themselves to the display of the carver's fantasies and abilities. These highly decorative objects would include girandoles, looking-glass frames, side and console tables and candlestands. Examples of all kinds and combinations of carving can be found on these pieces and, indeed, the carver's talents are wonderfully demonstrated.

FRETWORK

Fretwork should not be confused with pierced carving. Fretwork, i.e., perforated decoration, is indeed a form of openwork and sometimes is used in solid three-dimensional form—such as a fretwork stretcher on a Chinese Chippendale–style chair. However, fretwork, sometimes called cutwork, involves a technique of its own.

Fretwork is usually composed of small geometric interlacings, resembling trelliswork. In solid form, it serves as a structural detail—galleries for table tops and openwork stretchers for chairs and tables. As applied decoration to a solid ground (sometimes referred to as blind frets)—for friezes of tables and highboys and for chair legs during the vogues of the Chinese and Gothic Chippendale styles—fretwork served strictly as a form of applied ornamentation. Other forms of applied carved ornamentation are rosettes terminating the scrolls of a broken-scroll pedimented highboy, "streamer" carving on Philadelphia mid-18th-century rococo furniture, and many kinds of applied moldings. An example of applied fretwork for a frieze can be noted in illustration 74 on page 47. The tea table shown in illustration 91 displays a fretwork gallery.

Fretwork is occasionally cut out of the solid wood and as such is a straightforward form of incised geometric

90. *A carver's piece. One of a pair of
carved and gilded girandoles in the
18th-century English rococo style. It
closely follows the design of Plate No.
CLXXVIII in Thomas Chippendale's*
Gentleman & Cabinet-Maker's
Director *(3rd ed., 1762). Photograph
courtesy the Museum of Fine Arts,
Boston.*

carving. Some fretwork is cut from a single board; the design is cut out with a fret saw and then is glued onto its planned location. Most fretwork, however, is of laminated construction—three thicknesses of mahogany glued together. This lamination of three or more layers, with the grain of the center layer at right angles to the other two, created greater strength for the fragile fret. (See the close-up detail of the top of a fret gallery in illustration 91.) Lamination in this early form also lent its inherent stability, i.e., minimum movement, to these delicate constructions. Even so, it is rare to find structural fretwork totally intact without repairs and replacements.

91. Tea table with fretwork gallery. This early example of curving plywood construction provided important extra strength for the delicate fretwork gallery.

Chapter **7**

Nails and Screws

NAILS

Hand-Wrought Nails

FROM THE ROMAN HAND-FORGED "clavus" (found in excavations and sunken ships dating to 500 A.D.), through the 17th- and 18th-century "sparrabels," "clinkers" and "roses," and into the 19th century, nails were made by hand, one by one, by skilled "nailers." Furniture makers have always made occasional use of nails in their work. The first hand-wrought nails in the United States were imported from England, although, by the late 17th century, rolling and slitting mills which produced nail rods (rectangular strips or rods of malleable iron several feet long and about a quarter of an inch thick) had been built from Maine to Virginia.

The nail rods were cut and forged by hand into nails. The nailmaker, who may have been a professional or perhaps a farmer who needed nails to build a barn, heated one end of the nail rod in his forge and then, on the anvil, pointed it with the hammer on all four sides to the thickness and taper required. He then partly cut through the rod, above the point, inserted the pointed end in a hole of the proper size in a swage block, broke off the rod along the partial cutting, and hammered down the projecting end so as to spread it around the top of the hole to form a head. After the new nail cooled and shrank, it was easily knocked out of the swage block. The physical characterics of the handmade nail, therefore, are the roundish crested heads formed by hammer blows and the long, irregularly tapered squared shanks usually ending in points.

Many varieties and sizes of nails were wrought in this manner, ranging from huge spikes for shipbuilding to small nails for securing moldings and brasses on furniture. The furniture nail, less than 1″ in length and with a small flat head, or no head, is sometimes referred to as a "finish nail," and is relatively fine, as can be seen in the comparison photo (illustration 92). The names of other nail shapes include deck, clasp, cloat, cooper, clench, dog and horseshoe. Little evidence is available, however, for providing accurate dating for any of these variations.

Handmade nails were strong and tough and had long lives. The purity of the iron and the density of the texture (produced by hand-forging) made them highly resistant

92. *Early nails. Top to bottom, furniture-finishing nail with side-hammered L-shaped head; hand-wrought nail with convex-hammered-round head; cut-nail before hammered head application; cut-nail with square machine-stamped head, one operation.*

93. *Rough back of 18th-century chest of drawers secured to corestock with period nails. Note later but old canvas strip covering and holding the shrunken boards together.*

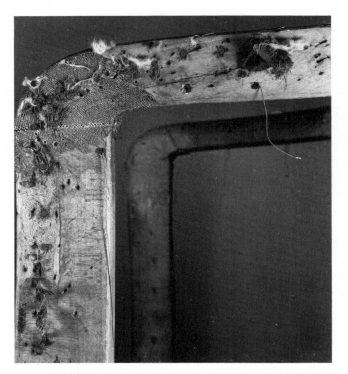

to rust and dampness, though they did bend in installation. Because of the time, effort and skill required to produce each nail, nails were a very precious commodity and the same nails were used again and again.

Hand-wrought nails are most often found in case pieces, particularly where early furniture makers used them to hold backboards in place. Early American Bible boxes, six-board chests, blanket chests and early drawers were usually nailed (see the 17th-century press cupboard drawer, illustration 63, page 41, and the nailed back side of the desk box, illustration 23, page 18), as were large architectural pieces such as corner cupboards. Nails were also used in the upholstering of chairs (see illustration 94) and as a means of decorating upholstery. This can be seen in the Copley portrait (see illustration 95) in which the artist confirms the use of large decorative brass nailheads to enhance the chair. Whenever old nails are found, they are helpful evidence in approximating the age of the piece because all nails were entirely hand-forged until almost 1800. For example, the likely date of the iron plate on the pedestal base of the tripod table (shown in illustration 123, page 80) is reinforced by the likely date of supporting nails.

Cut-Nails

The more easily produced machine-cut nail, called a cut-nail, superseded the use of wrought nails everywhere by the early 1800s because it was so much cheaper. Two cut-nail factories had been established in Philadelphia by 1797. The cut-nail consists of a rectangular tapering shank of iron, not hammered into a point by hand, but tapered by a single angle cut across a plate of iron. The blacksmith was thus furnished with a strip of plate iron, several feet in length, about 2¼″ wide and usually about ⅛″ thick. The strip slid into a cutter, which, rising and falling rapidly, clipped off the end of the iron plate crosswise into narrow tapering rectangular slices—or nails. The taper of the cut produced the point of a nail. The nailhead was made by dropping the freshly cut piece, point downward, into a slotted clamp or vise, and then spreading the larger projecting end with a hammer as in the case of the wrought nail. Hammer-headed cut-nails thus required two operations. They date from 1800–1825 and hence are occasionally found used in furniture made during that time.

94. *A barrel-back English Hepplewhite-style chair frame, stripped of its upholstery. In the wing upper-corner detail, many rows of irregular and square-shaped tack holes can be seen, made by wrought and cut-iron upholstery tacks of the past—a chair of this date, about 1795, would have likely been reupholstered several times in its history.*

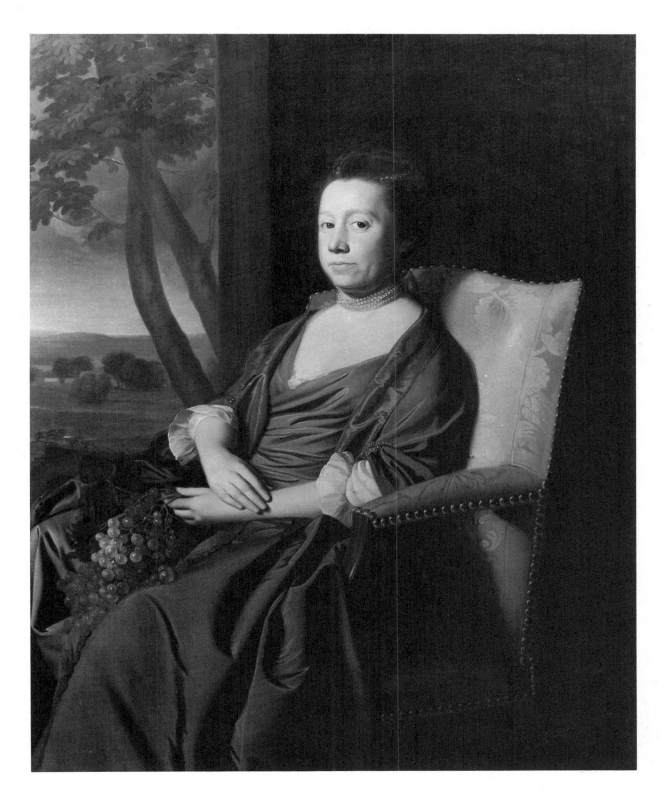

95. Portrait of Mrs. Isaac Smith by John Singleton Copley, painted in 1769. Large brass nailheads were used to ornament 18th-century richly upholstered armchairs. Eighteenth-century brass upholstery nails were single sand-mold cast pieces, whereas their modern counterparts are made in two pieces, a wire shank and a stamped head. Photograph courtesy the Yale University Art Gallery. Gift of Maitland Fuller Griggs.

96. Nail forms. The hand-wrought nail (a) tapers on four sides; the cut-nail (b) tapers on two opposite sides; the machine-made wire nail (c) has a circular shank and tapers continuously.

By 1825, the cut-nail machine had been perfected so as to enable cut-nails to be made by a single operation in one machine, in which the machine cut the nail, clamped it and, in a single blow of great pressure to the end of the nail, formed the head by the displacement of metal. The earliest stamped heads (1825–1830) were thin, lopsided and imperfect but became thicker, square and more regular after 1830.

Both hammer-headed cut-nails and machine-headed cut-nails are easily distinguished from hand-wrought nails. Cut and wrought nails both have rectangular shanks, but the wrought nails taper on four sides—the cut-nail only on two opposite sides. The cut-nail will be as thick at the point as at the head—in fact the thickness of the nail plate from which it was cut. Furthermore, the two cut sides of the cut-nail show minute parallel striations or burrs, absent on the wrought nail, which mark the down smear of the cutter. However, it is interesting to note that the newly invented cut-nail was too brittle to clench and could not compete with the strength of its handmade predecessor for such things as gates, doors, wagon bodies and boats; thus hand-forged nail production continued for another century.

In about 1870, the modern, machine-made steel wire nail with its round head and circular shank made its general appearance. It was manufactured earlier in the 19th century in Europe, but American wire-nail machinery was not perfected until the 1860s—machinery for this purpose was exhibited at the 1876 Centennial Exhibition in Philadelphia. The earliest wire nails can be distinguished from their modern counterparts by their heads being bulbous and generally eccentric with respect to their shanks. Wire nails do not represent age earlier than the late 19th century, and when found in a seemingly older piece of furniture, indicate late 19th- or 20th-century repairs, alterations, or maintenance.

SCREWS

Handmade Screws

Screws were handmade as of about 1700 and were much more scarce than nails during the 18th century. The cutting of the thread without the benefit of steel dies required a great deal of time, patience and skill, making screws a very expensive item for the provincial cabinet-maker. When the machine-cut screw made its appearance around 1812, it not only proved cheaper, but was more effective, thereby bringing handmade production to a quick end.

Screws, as well as nails, are a guide to dates and thus age. Eighteenth-century screws were handmade and can be easily recognized. Studying an early iron or brass screw, one can see that the spiral thread of the shank (sometimes called the worm) was hand-cut with a file. The threads are thus uneven and rounded rather than sharp. There is practically no taper to the shaft and the ends were cut off square. The slots in the hand-filed heads, made with a hacksaw, were shallow, narrow, irregular and sometimes slightly off center, as opposed to the spun head of the modern screw. This handmade screw is compared with a modern screw in illustrations 97 and 98.

Early handmade screws with their extra strength capacity (when compared with nails) had many important uses. Table tops have always been attached to their frames or legs with screws. (Note the old screws in the underside of the table in illustration 179, page 125.) All hinges required and contained screws since screws, unlike nails, did not need clinching (i.e., turning over the point) to hold the hinge and thus did not disfigure the top surface on drop-leaf tables and other concealed hinge locations. (See the hinge in illustration 108, page 72.) Locks were secured with screws. The backs of case pieces were sometimes screwed rather than nailed to the core stock. Chest-of-drawer tops were often screwed down. Obviously all screw-in knobs involved screws—the tiny brass knobs on the little drawers behind the hinged slant lid of an 18th-century desk come to mind. Cornerblocks, important in the construction of chairs, were sometimes screwed into place.

Machine-Cut Screws

The machine-cut metal screw was made for a short time between 1815 and 1845. This was a relatively uniform screw with a blunt end, even screw threads and a round even head. Made in a factory with steam-engine power, there were five operations involved: the cutting of the wire to the correct length, the forging of the head, the turning of the head and upper part of the shank, the cutting of the notch and the cutting of the thread.

The modern "gimlet-point" (pointed-end) metal screw dates from the Great Exhibition of 1851. Modern metal screws in old furniture therefore suggest either replacement or that the piece was made after 1851. The screws securing a hinge or lock are likely to be replaced; elsewhere, replacement is less probable. The likelihood of a screw which has been in place for a century or more coming loose and falling out, thus requiring replacement

97. *Handmade (left) and modern (right) screws showing head slots.*

98. *Left: Handmade screw.*
Right: Modern "gimlet-point" screw.

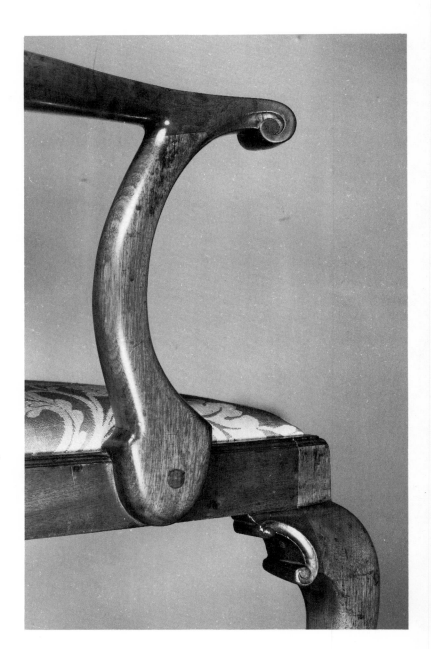

99. *Detail of armchair showing use of the wooden plug to disguise the screw head. Earlier 18th-century cabinetmakers generally used screws from the inside out; hence there would have been no need for such concealment.*

by a modern screw, is remote without special movement at that part. Replacement screws are relatively easy to remove, and upon examination of the hole from which the screw has been removed, two sets of screw threads should be apparent, proving the replacement of an earlier screw. Furthermore, screws, like nails, rust with changes in temperature and humidity; hence early screws will have stained the wood around them. Note the 17th-century drawer nail and the surrounding wood (illustration 63, page 41).

It should be observed that on a good piece of furniture no two screws (or nails) will be inserted on the same line, a precaution taken to avoid splitting the wood along the lines of its grain. It should also be noted that 18th-century cabinetmakers used colored beeswax to conceal screw heads and nailheads. The Victorian cabinetmakers preferred wooden plugs for this purpose, attempting to match the direction of the grain, color and wood of the plug to the surround as much as possible. An example of such a wooden plug can be seen in the photographed Chippendale-style chair (illustration 99) where the arm support is screwed to the seat rail.

8

Hardware and Accessories

FURNITURE HARDWARE AND ACCESSORIES provide an interesting source of supporting information as to the age of a piece of furniture. They should always receive careful examination by the student of antique furniture.

HINGES

Hinges are a basic functional element in the construction of furniture, at the same time often serving as a means of decoration.

Pin Hinge and Strap Hinge

Wooden pin hinges date back to 12th- and 13th-century chests. Hand-wrought iron hinges were also in general use at that time, particularly for heavily strapped chests (see illustration 7, page 10), some of the straps on the lid being finished off to form part of the hinge. The oldest type of strap hinge did not have a pin; the tongue was simply pulled through a slot in the shorter plate and bent over. (This is sometimes described as the wrapped joint

of such a hinge.) However, by the middle of the 18th century, the strong strap hinges were made with pins and continue in this basic form today. Strap hinges, often with chamfered edges—especially in England—are known in many shapes. The "cocks-head" shaped hinge of 17th-century England and the "H" and "L" hinges of 18th-century England and Colonial America are examples.

Cotter-Pin Hinge

Large cotter pins of hand-wrought iron, linked together by inserting one through the loop of the other (sometimes called staple hinges), were another early form of hinge often used for the lids of blanket chests and Bible boxes, primarily in the late 17th century and some in the early 18th century. The pairs of pointed ends, made from the interlocking iron loops, went through the top and back of a chest and were turned over or "clinched" into the wood. This was not a terribly durable arrangement, though simple and serviceable, and most of these hinges worked loose or broke. Evidence of their earlier presence often remains, and this is a welcome sign of authenticity.

100. Wooden pin hinge.

101. Wrought-iron strap hinge.

102. Iron cotter-pin hinge or staple hinge.

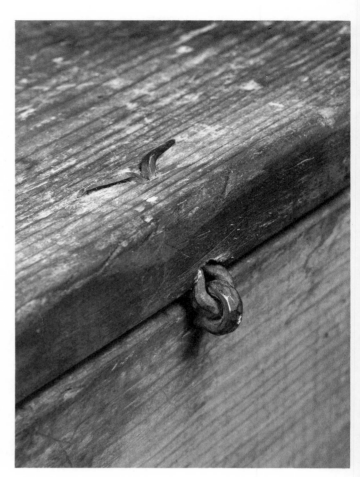

103. Cotter-pin hinge showing ends "clinched" into the wood.

104. Butterfly hinge.

105. Wrought-iron butterfly hinge used to fasten the slanting top and flat top of a 17th-century oak desk box in the Jacobean style. (Note the replacement modern screw.)

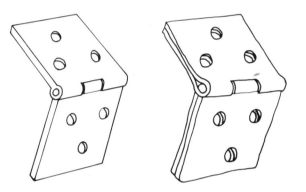

106. Modern rectangular iron hinge stamped from a single thickness of metal (left) and hand-wrought double-thickness iron hinge (right).

107. Elaborate iron hinge with end bent double.

Butterfly Hinge

So-called because the leaves when open flare out from the pin like the wings of a butterfly, the butterfly hinge was widely used up through 1750 and often had edges that were thinner than the main body of the hinge, i.e., the metal was drawn toward the extremities, leaving the greater thickness against the hinge. This feature was produced by hammering on an anvil. The holes in the butterfly hinge were never perfectly round because they were punched in by the blacksmith while the wings of the hinges were hot and before their edges were rolled over the center pin.

Rectangular Butt Hinges

Forms of rectangular hinges can be found used on furniture from the 17th century onward. The halves of the early hand-forged hinge are often of two thicknesses and slightly irregular. That is to say that a blacksmith has taken a thin strip of wrought iron, bent it double, and welded it together. The inner edge (the joint) is thus left rounded for the insertion of the pin which unites the two parts. A comparison of such an old hinge with a relatively modern one is made in illustration 106. Again, such hinges were usually attached with clinched nails or rivets. The later machine-made iron hinge has rectangular plates stamped from a single thickness of metal, and the circular opening for the pin is evenly formed by curling one side of the plate. The 18th-century Dawes cellarette shown here (illustration 108) has an elaborately shaped hinge with part bent double surrounding the pin.

Brass Hinges

Old brass butt hinges were made by hand-casting the leaves (plates) from molten metal. Slight imperfections in the shape and surface are therefore evident, and the back sides will be pitted. Modern ones are machine-stamped from sheets of rolled brass, bent to receive the iron hinge pin. Hence new brass hinges are much smoother and certainly much stronger.

Hardware and Accessories · 71

108. *Hinged late 18th-century Continental cellarette which belonged to the patriot William Dawes, who rode with Paul Revere on the night of April 18, 1775.*

109. *Hand-wrought iron hasp lock, drawn from a 15th-century European bridal casket.*

LOCKS

More than an accessory for decoration, locks have always served an important function as a means of security. Going back to the 14th century in Europe, chests were fitted with one or more hand-wrought iron locks. The movement (or works) of these early locks was sunk into the woodwork, and the face-plate was therefore flush with the surface of the chest. The hasp (the separate overlaid member) was hinged to its supporting metal strap, usually on the lid of the chest. Such hasp locks in their plain, rectangular form are common to chests and boxes of all periods.

Compact small brass locks for drawers of chests, cabinet doors and the fall fronts of desks gradually evolved from the large, often highly complicated and elaborate iron locks used on medieval chests and other receptacles. In fact, few drawers in the 18th century were without locks. Again the works were embedded into the woodwork; a French or Continental lock mechanism was generally let into a slot in the front of the drawer; whereas the usual English and American practice was to cut a slot for a lock on the back side so it lay flush with the back of the drawer front. Squared locks with centered keyholes on drawer fronts usually indicate Continental work, whereas the standard English/American square brass lock frame is mounted near the top center edge of a drawer. A French lock turns clockwise twice for locking pins to be fully home; an English or American lock turns anticlockwise and is fully bolted with one turn.

A covering decorative escutcheon plate (such as seen in illustration 110, page 74, or the drawer escutcheon plate in illustration 148, page 104) was placed over the keyhole on the front surface. The keyhole to the lock is simply outlined on the surface of the late 18th-century drawer fronts with inlaid brass stringing (see illustration 8, page 11). During the mid-18th century, especially in France, the key sometimes served as a handle, no other handles being provided.

Sheraton in his *Cabinet Dictionary* of 1803 described the various kinds of locks used for cabinetwork accordingly: "Of this useful instrument of security, there are various species. The common till lock, both spring and tumbler, used for drawers. The cupboard door kind, common, and spring and tumbler, used for bookcase and wardrobe doors. Box locks with link plates, such as for tea chests and wine cisterns. Mortice locks, some for doors, and others for sliders of cylindrical writing tables. Those for inner doors are called spring locks, and are the most considerable, both in use and structure. The principal parts of a spring lock are the main plate, the cover plate, and the pin hole; to the main plate belong the key hole, top hook, cross wards, bolt toe, draw back spring, tumbler, pin of the tumbler, and the staples; to the cover plate belong the pin, main ward, cross ward, step ward, or dap ward; to the pin hole belong the hook ward, main cross ward shank, the pot or broad bow ward and the bit."

Occasionally a lock is found stamped with a crown, the initial of the British reigning monarch, "WR" (William Rex) or "VR" (Victoria Regina), and the maker's name with the word "Patent" in capitals, a practice which began in the mid-19th century. The more important lock patentees included Bramah, Barron and Chubb. The maker's name was often omitted on early Victorian locks, however, and these were usually stamped with the crown and cypher and the words "Patent Secure Lever Lock," or something similar. Should one observe the marks of a file or emery wheel on either side of the levers, it is likely that the lock once had a Victorian name or patent which has been rubbed away to imply greater age. Locks are subject to wear and damage to such an extent that they are frequently changed or removed.

BRASSES

Brasses, metal mounts made of brass, provide magnificent accent and decoration for a piece of furniture. At the same time they are useful as handles for drawers and doors or for the sides of heavy case pieces to accommodate lifting and carrying. Brasses must also be appreciated as a feat of remarkable craftsmanship and beauty in their own right. Styling is a most important consideration,

and brasses have varied in style and material as the furniture itself has changed in style over periods of time.

Collectors in general take delight in examining a piece which still has its "original brasses," the brass mounts which were originally made or intended for the piece and the only ones it has ever had. However, this is not often the situation, as there are many reasons why the original brasses have, over the years, been removed and replaced. Changes in fashion would account for the disappearance of many, for owners wishing to be up-to-date would have the prevailing style fitted to furniture of an earlier date. The simple fact that brasses could be changed may well have tempted some owners to exchange their brasses for a later or earlier style of greater personal preference. In some other cases, original handles would get broken or become detached and lost due to natural wear and tear. Often an entire set of new brasses was fitted, this being less trouble than having one or two reproduced from those that remained.

When looking at a brass, immediate concern should be directed toward the encrustation which surrounds it. If this encrustation appears intact, i.e., the buildup of dirt, wax and dust around it appears undisturbed, there is good reason to believe that the brass is old and perhaps original to the piece. If an old brass is removed, the encrustation should contrast markedly with the exposed wood surface and the undisturbed wood beneath the brass. This undisturbed wood should appear quite beautiful due to the patina having developed without interruption. Encrustation can be recognized surrounding the escutcheon plate in illustration 110.

At the time the encrustation is being noted, doors and drawers should be examined for signs of having been fitted with other (and perhaps earlier) brasses. For example, on the drawer front there may be faint outlines of encrustation not matching the outline of the present brasses. (Outlines of earlier brasses may be detected despite refinishing because of the difference in patina resulting from the exposed and covered wood surfaces.) Another sign to look for is wooden plugs filling holes made by the posts and nuts of earlier brasses. Examination of a piece's interior may reveal unexplained holes and other marks where different brasses were once attached. The pictured drawer interior (see illustration 111) is a typical sample of unqualified holes—and hence earlier brasses than the present.

In examining brasses, it should be kept in mind that all old brasses have a mellow surface patina which one comes to recognize with experience. The face of a 17th- or 18th-century brass is never completely smooth despite polishing, and this can be quickly ascertained by running one's finger across the face of several brasses in the same set. These old brasses have been cast by a craftsman and

110. *Escutcheon plate surrounded by encrustation.*

111. *Drawer with unqualified holes and marks inside the drawer front. Corner joinery hand-saw overcuts can also be observed.*

112. *Face of a mid-18th-century hand-cast brass plate with its parts. Note slight imperfections due to hand craftsmanship.*

113. *Rough back side of hand-cast brass plate.*

consequently slight variables caused by his hand and materials will be present. First, the designer or carver made the model, then the molder made the mold and poured in the hot metal, and finally the chaser or finisher cut away the faults in the casting, filed up the edges and polished the surfaces. The remaining subtle surface "waves," so delightful today, can be seen with the aid of a bright light, as well as felt. Other marks of hand craftsmanship (casting flaws, bubbles, etc.) can also be detected in this manner. Study the early brasses (illustrations 112 and 113). Queen Anne–style brasses which were chased by hand with a set of punches and special chisels will each be slightly different; the chasing will vary to a small extent from plate to plate, and the plate outline is also likely to vary due to hand trimming and finishing.

The back side of the cast brass plate was not finished or polished, and it is therefore most important to examine this surface for the telltale signs of rough pitted grain from the sand mold. It is again interesting to note that many seemingly flat brasses are, in fact, uneven on the front and on the back due to the early crude methods of production. (Modern reproduction plates are usually cut from sheet brass and are thus smooth and even on the back.)

Plates and Pulls

After consideration of the brass surfaces, the inside of the drawer should be explored to see how the brass has been attached to the drawer, this being of great significance in determining age. On early pieces that date from the late 17th century, the plates are flat, plain and thin. The small drop handles or pulls are fastened with a flat wire, called a cotter pin, placed through a loop at the end of the pull, the two ends of the wire then being passed through a hole in the plate and the front of the drawer before being bent back on the drawer interior, just like a cotter-pin hinge. Incidentally, the pear-shaped pulls found on doors and drawers of late 17th-century furniture are invariably hollow or flat at the back; that is, they were only half the

Hardware and Accessories · 75

114. *Late 17th-century tear-drop pull.*

115. *Early 18th-century pull in the Queen Anne style.*

shape of the pear. This form remained in use for nearly a century, after which the whole pear shape was cast.

At the end of the 17th century an entirely new form of cabinet mount, the loop (or bail) handle with a shaped flat plate, often engraved and chamfer-edged, became the standard type and remained so throughout the first half of the 18th century. An example of this is the Queen Anne pull. The only connecting link between this new mount and its predecessor, the small drop, was the manner of fixing the handle to the plate by two iron or brass cotter pins. This double-cotter-pin method gave way to the use of a cast knob, a part of the backplate into which the ends of the loop handle were engaged (see drawing of bat-wing brass, illustration 116). These knobs formed the face of the bolts whose cast square posts (or shanks) secured the backplate to the drawer by means of hand-filed threads and small, oddly shaped, rough cast metal nuts (see illustrations 116 and 117). (In reproductions, the posts are round, the threads are machined and the nuts are larger and exactly square.) Old versus new nuts can be easily checked by inspecting the nuts on the inner side of the drawer where the posts come through from the front. Old nuts are cast as odd bits of brass tapped to fit loosely on the crude threads, and probably will fit only that particular post.

The loop handle also shows a rather distinct change in the first half of the 18th century. In its earliest form, the handle was slim, with the ends curving inward and ending in knobs which enabled them to be held in

position by metal cotter pins. The wrought-iron handle on the hide trunk (illustration 121, page 79) follows this same simple shape. With the passing of the cotter-pin fixing, the loop was hung from the inner sides of the knobs and ornamented by a baluster-like detail in the center (see illustration 115). The baluster was later replaced with a plain heavy swelling, the ends of the handles curving inward.

A further use of the loop handle in this form developed after the publication of Chippendale's *Director* in 1754 when the backplate was replaced by two small round or elliptical brasses made of cast brass with decorative grooved or bead-molded edges to which each end of the bail handle joined. The hole in the rosette plate was square, thus fitting the square shank of the post.

During the early 18th century the backplates, keyhole escutcheon plates, etc., were fixed to the drawer and door fronts with small round-headed brass pins. Screws were in use, but the proper equipment to make them sufficiently small for this use was lacking.

About 1780, backplates were no longer cast and chased, nor ornamented with piercing, but instead made of thin rolled sheet brass stamped in relief. The bail handle became wider and hooked on to the post heads from the outside. (See drawing of Hepplewhite-style brass, illustration 118.) On fine delicate furniture, brasses or pulls of this type were sometimes of silver. Some metal backplates appearing between 1775 and 1800 were pressed into dies and the hollow at the back was filled in with composition. Pattern variety was great, including patriotic elliptical plates, geometric medallions and symbolic designs of thistles, doves and conch shells. The diemakers of the period were skilled craftsmen producing sharply defined designs. It should be remembered that old posts were hand-cast, whereas reproductions are usually machine-turned from round stock.

Following the Hepplewhite- and Sheraton-style elliptical- and rectangular-shaped brasses, round brass knobs served as handles for drawers and doors. Again, they were usually stamped from sheet brass and filled with composition to add weight and strength. The screw was soldered directly to the knob, thereby eliminating separate posts. This unit held the backplate in position on the front and a nut screwed on the back held the brass knob secure to the wood (see illustration 119). Notice how the wood has been cut away directly around the screw at the

116. *Mid-18th-century bat-wing brass.*

117. *Late 18th-century/early 19th-century loop handle with rosette backplates.*

118. *Late 18th-century/early 19th-century stamped-brass backplate.*

119. *Early 19th-century brass knob.*

back, thereby counter-sinking this detail and protecting it from activity in the drawer, at the same time protecting the contents of the drawer from damage by snagging.

Final observations in our consideration of brasses should include the importance given to chamfering the edges of these mounts. Stop-chamfering, or irregular cutting of the front surface edges, was also employed. (Often "cocks-head" hinges are found with stop-chamfering.) In the course of carefully scrutinizing sets of mounts to determine their age and place of origin, one often amusingly discovers that the cabinetmaker has had to "make do" with the brasses he had on hand for his current work. Naturally, he did not want to waste his existing supply and thus one occasionally finds much earlier-style brasses used on a piece of furniture of far later style. Because brasses in Colonial America were primarily imported from England, what arrived was of course used—regardless of size and shape. Thus, for example, pieces of furniture in the Karolik Collection at the Museum of Fine Arts in Boston contain brasses which have been cut away or bent in order to fit into the available and planned area for each brass. So important a piece as the shell-carved Newport desk-and-bookcase (illustration 120) has imported "make-do" cut-down and overlapping brasses on its hinged slant lid.

120. *"Make-do" brass on hinged slant lid of mahogany Townsend-Goddard School desk-and-bookcase, circa 1760–1775. (The terms "secretary" and "secretary-bookcase" by which this form is commonly known today were introduced in England only in the 1780s to describe desks in which the writing surface is provided not by the hinged slant-front lid but by the unfolded front of the upper drawer; hence, desk-and-bookcase is the more accurate term.)*

GILT-BRONZE

Many brass and bronze mounts were gilded, particularly those in the mid-18th-century rococo style of France. This was done for additional beauty and to protect the metal against tarnishing. Work treated thus is called ormolu in England and the process was as follows: Mercury was heated in a crucible and, at the necessary temperature, pure gold was added. Upon forming an amalgam, the mixture was allowed to cool. The resulting paste was laid out on flat surface and applied to the cast-metal mount with a wire brush, the article thus appearing to be painted silver. Washed and subjected to burning temperature, which caused the mercury to dissipate in fumes, the gold was left fast, ready for polishing or burnishing. The French excelled in this technique.

IRON MOUNTS

Iron mounts have played a simple but important role in furniture history. Like the brass mounts, they perform the utilitarian function of handles for opening doors and drawers and for lifting and carrying pieces. They were usually hand-wrought, the work of the ordinary blacksmith. Hence they were simple hammered forgings with the occasional use of the punch, chisel and file for decoration and attempted smoothness. These straightforward mounts were intended for simple pieces of furniture such as country case furniture and utilitarian kitchen pieces (see illustration 121). The most elaborately decorated examples of wrought-iron mounts can be seen on medieval European chests and trunks.

Wrought-iron forgings were also used as braces or supports for parts of furniture where weakness was present or likely to occur. Therefore, supporting pieces of hand-wrought iron can be found anywhere on a piece. The early age of the iron piece is recognized by its uneven hammered surface, the shape of its outline, and the fact that it is attached with old nails or screws. Frequently, iron plates can be found under the pedestal of 18th-century tripod tea tables, helping to support the joint where the three legs join the center pedestal. Any pressure on the table top is a threat to the three small legs being forced out of their joints, hence a reinforcing iron plate, or "Y-brace," helps to keep them safely in place.

121. *Simple hand-forged iron handle on a late 18th-century hide trunk (the hide being used to repel water).*

CASTORS

Small solid wheels attached to the lower extremities of a piece of furniture, enabling it to move without having to be lifted, seem to have been used in England as far back as the end of the 17th century. On the Continent they were used even earlier.

Early furniture incorporated hardwood wheels which were unable to swivel about a vertical axis. This shortcoming was remedied in the early 18th century when castors were introduced. They were secured into sockets with pins which allowed them to move in all directions, and early examples consisted of a boxwood ball running on a metal axle. This form was soon superseded by a boxwood roller. About 1750, leather castors came into use on high-fashion furniture, a number of leather discs

being strung together on the axle and held in position by brass "horns" attached to a flat metal plate. (The metal core fit up into the leg and was not visible.)

By 1770, castors made of brass (see illustration 32, page 22), with cup- or box-type fittings which encased the leg, were available in trade catalogs in three styles, each in many stock sizes. Sheraton's *Cabinet Dictionary* illustrates several types of brass castor. He also lists castors for bedposts. In Regency-period tables the toe-cap castor often took the shape of a lion's-paw foot of brass or the surfaces were decorated with honeysuckle, acanthus or other designs in relief, some of these paw castors containing several wheels. During the Victorian years, white ceramic castors were produced and used on chairs and small tables. The brass platform castor with hollow brass rollers is also 19th-century, often found on parlor chairs in the Rococo-revival style.

122. Bottom of the central pedestal of a tripod table showing how the legs are slot-dovetail joined into the pedestal. Note the wood-splitting damage to the sides of the joint that occurs when downward pressure comes from the table top, producing side leverage.

123. Reinforcing hand-wrought iron plate found at the base of a tripod table pedestal.

124. A leather castor circa 1760 showing the leather three-section roller. Leather castors were desirable because they did not scratch the floor.

124. A leather castor circa 1760 showing the leather three-section roller. Leather castors were desirable because they did not scratch the floor.

GLASS

Glass, particularly in the form of bookcase-door glasses and looking glasses, is an important factor in establishing the authenticity of old furniture. It was well into the latter part of the 19th century before the art of making perfectly flat sheet glass in large sizes was developed.

With its many imperfections, 18th-century glass is easily recognizable. Anyone with the good fortune to possess examples, whether in the form of a looking glass, in windows in an historic house, or as part of a piece of furniture, should treat them with great care. Old glass is extremely brittle! Due to methods of manufacture (blowing and casting), old glass is of unequal thickness, never truly flat and often curved. These characteristics provide a pleasing play of light on the panes, though there is some distortion of objects seen through the glass. This unevenness (bumpiness, imperfections and occasional air bubbles) can actually be felt. Old glass will always have a greenish, bluish or brownish color cast.

Looking glasses of polished metal or silvered glass have been highly prized from very early times. Small looking glasses, chiefly from Venice, were imported into England early in the 15th century. The making of silvered glass became an established industry in England during the reign of William and Mary (1689–1702) and heavy duties on glass were imposed in 1695. These duties affected America as an English colony by severely curtailing the use of glass in bookcase doors and other furniture—as well as for architectural purposes. (Windows were few and small until after the Revolution.)

Glass plates of any size were very expensive to make, and the best were generally imperfect. The old silvering for looking glasses was done by the mercury process, where quicksilver was "floated" on the back of glass, adhering only by its cohesion with a perfect surface. Quicksilver, being heavy, would be liable to fall off if the glass had any irregularities (and old glass is rarely perfect), so that today the silvering on old looking glasses is always spotted, fogged or missing in several areas. In addition, as the mercury is on the back, any discoloration of the glass itself was noticeable on the front; 18th-century glass usually has a bluish tinge.

125. Ceramic castor, mid-19th-century English drop-leaf table.

Today the silvering of mirrors is done by the "patent" process, with silver foil used in place of mercury. A good test for an old looking glass, even if it has been resilvered (and by the "patent" method), is to hold up a sheet of white paper to it and observe the reflection—the blue tint of the old glass becomes apparent at once.

Truly old silvered glass remains difficult to detect, however, as the mercury process is still done on fakes. When mercury is applied to glass with an uneven back, it will soon fog and spot. The old bevels are also carefully imitated. Both the genuine and the fake bevels differ from the modern in being very broad and shallow with a very subtle demarcation line between the bevel and the face of the glass, almost as if they had been molded with the glass instead of being ground with a sand-wheel. Bevelled glass is characteristic of period Queen Anne looking glasses and its flatness is due in part to the great thinness of the glass at that time.

126. Early 19th-century breakfront bookcase door of contemporary glass panes. Note the imperfections in the glass.

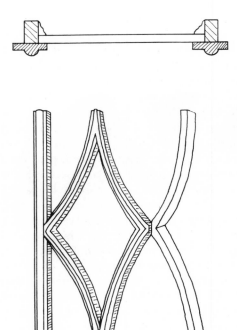

127. Arrangement for setting the individual panes of glass into the molding tracery of a glazed bookcase door. Each pane, cut to the appropriate shape, is positioned against the back side of the astragal molding and held in place with putty.

Chapter **9**

Finish

FINISH ON A PIECE of furniture is often loosely described as its patina. All finishes have patinas, and all patinas are to some extent the product of the furniture finishes. However, the two words are not synonymous.

PATINA

"Patina" is a word used to describe a desirable old furniture surface condition, a soft, warm, mellow look which comes with age and circumstances. The quality of furniture patina depends upon the care a piece has received, its situation and the conditions to which it has been exposed during its lifetime.

The purest definition of patina would be the act of simple oxidation of raw wood over time. This alone, without the addition of such outside elements as stain, wax and dirt, will give wood a "smoked" color and tone. The rafters in an old barn serve as a case in point. Once the barn has been completed, the rafters remain untouched. Yet fifty or a hundred years later, they will appear "smoky" and weathered as the result of oxidation, the wood's interaction with the atmosphere. Secondary surfaces on pieces of furniture will have this same look—the bottoms of drawers and the backs of case pieces, for example. This "old" look is in obvious contrast to the looks and feel of a new piece of wood and it is virtually impossible to imitate.

The word patina is usually *not* used in reference to secondary wood surfaces on furniture, but is reserved for primary surfaces. In addition to undergoing the process of normal oxidation, a primary furniture surface has likely been stained and possibly treated with some finish as well. Over time, this surface has been waxed, rubbed (causing gentle friction), oiled, polished, dirtied, worn and at times inadvertently allowed to fade from exposure through a sunny window. The handsome result is what is commonly meant by the word patina.

True patina is by far the most beautiful and appealing single feature found in an old piece of furniture. It is impossible to reproduce, although attempts are made. After careful examination of true patinated surfaces, and a basic knowledge of the typical old finishes and their behavior over time, one can usually detect questionable patina.

128. *Door of an early 17th-century cupboard from Dalecarlia, Sweden. The brightly colored painting is dated 1813.*

KINDS OF FINISH

Finishing treatments have always been used on furniture and these so-called "finishes," each with its own characteristics, strengths and weaknesses, have served as a protection and preservative to the piece of furniture. The beauty of the piece—its wood figure, its proportions, its decorative detail—has been enhanced throughout with the application of one or more finishes to its primary surfaces.

Obviously, many things are likely to have happened to a piece of furniture over its history. Since surface finish is highly vulnerable to change and damage, this makes determining original finish or the history of a piece's finish extremely challenging. One could easily find that an 18th-century piece which was originally oiled or waxed (the two most common finishes at that time owing to availability and cheapness) had been French-polished later and, afterwards, rewaxed. Sometimes only parts have been treated in this way—a badly marked table top may have been stripped down and French-polished, for instance, and the remainder left untouched. Most varnished and shellacked 18th-century furniture has most likely been refinished several times since it was made.

Paint

A simple kind of finish and one easily accessible to all cabinetmakers was milk paint. (Sour milk and rust provided a red color, for example.) This proved an attractive and protective finish with such colorful results as green or black Windsor chairs and painted, decorated Pennsylvania Dutch chests. Sometimes they were most extravagant in their painted detail—as in the 17th-century Swedish cupboard pictured here (illustration 128), which was painted in 1813. Paint covered up any imperfections in the wood, such as knotholes. (In fact, if a piece was made of pine, it was usually painted.) Paint as a finish also disguised the cabinetmaker's use of several woods in the same piece of furniture (again the Windsor chair comes to mind), and it proved to be indeed durable as verified by the many early pieces extant today (even allowing for the recent fashion of stripping such pieces and refinishing with varnish or shellac).

The approximate age of paint can be established. Old paint, 100 years or older, is tenacious. It is brittle and extremely difficult to remove. This is because over time oxidation has taken place and the natural oils in the paint have evaporated; the paint actually shrinks, sometimes with a resulting appearance of crazing (fine hairline cracks) or overall cracking (more severe fracturing). A quick test for age is to scratch the paint surface with a knife. The paint will shatter if old. However, if it is new and still contains its natural oils, it will roll off in curls much like the curled shavings from a plane. Given current aesthetic interest in historic paint, and therefore the increased value of a piece with original paint, a black light can be used to confirm the age of the paint. (New paint will fluoresce bright purple.)

Varnish

Varnish, which dates back to ancient Egyptian use, is a strong finish used on all types and most styles of furniture. Generally it is water- and alcohol-resistant and thus a very durable and practical finish. The shortcoming of varnish is the opaque hairline checking, sometimes called "alligatoring" because of its crackle appearance, which occurs in the course of time (see illustration 41, page 29). Although the presence of alligatoring is an excellent indication that the varnish finish is indeed old, it obscures the figure and color of the wood, giving the piece a cold, dull appearance. There is no way to revive an old crackle varnish finish.

A test of an old varnish is to rub a small surface area with sandpaper. Because the natural oils will have dried (oxidized) in old varnish, the finish will powder when sanded. In contrast, a very new varnish finish will roll off in curls when sanded because little oxidation has taken place.

129. Tall clock case providing a dramatic example of "alligatored" old varnish.

A further test for determining a varnish finish (as opposed to shellac, for example) is to apply a small amount of alcohol to an obscure area of the finish. If the finish does not react (i.e., if it withstands the alcohol), it is very likely that the piece has been finished with varnish, not shellac (shellac will dissolve with alcohol).

Copal varnishes were probably the most common hard-resin fixed-oil varnishes used in the 18th century, partly because of their extreme hardness and durability and partly because they were "white," lacking the amber color of most resin varnishes. Copal varnishes, so-called "Vernis Martin," gained renown from their development and use by the famous Martin brothers of Paris.

Shellac

Shellac is a hard and durable organic finish. Shellac gums are derived from the exudation of the lac insect (a scale insect, related to the aphids), which lives on the twigs of certain trees. These gums are cut (mixed) with alcohol to form a ready-to-use finish. The most resilient of all finishes, shellac will take much abuse and wear. It is also the most challenging finish to apply properly to a furniture surface, as it must be laid on smoothly, with even continuous motion, and in correct quantity the first time. Problems with brush strokes, bubbles, etc., can only be corrected by sanding off that coat and redoing it. Since it dries quickly, the finisher must also work with speed. Shellac can be applied with a brush but is usually applied by the French-polish method using a cloth pad (called "ragging"). The end result is unrivalled for its beauty, luster and sheen after rubbing by hand. One cabinetmaker who works frequently with both varnish and shellac likens varnish to maple syrup, and shellac to whipped cream.

Shellac is likely to be the finish used on all important hardwood pieces of furniture starting in the early 19th century and is very much the preference of furniture connoisseurs today. However, since shellac is vulnerable to heat, water and alcohol, shellacked furniture must receive mindful care and protection.

130. Cabriole leg showing color variation due to end-grain exposure.

Oil

The oiled finish simply involves repeated applications of oil to the raw wood surface, which soon produces a finished look and some protection for the wood. Repeated applications will continue to darken the wood; the result is not reversible. Alas, the use of combined linseed oil and turpentine for care of old pieces of furniture has been a widespread practice.

Stain

Another straightforward method of finishing a piece was to stain it and then follow this with a coat of beeswax and turpentine. Stains are preparations which are thinner than paint and are thus absorbed by wood pores without forming a coating. Early stains provide interesting study, as almost anything was used—berries, animal urine, walnut extract made from boiling walnut shells, syrups, dragon's blood made from tree bark, ground roots and chemicals (sulphuric acid, vinegar, ammonia, copper sulfate, coal tar, etc.). Tea was an especially good dye for oak. If a chemical stain has been used on the wood, the wood will *never* fade in sunlight; if anything, it will get darker. Hence, some early mahogany chairs are almost black. Contrarily, if the stain is organic or natural (derived from animals or plants), it will fade with sun exposure and time. This latter effect is the most desirable by today's standards of beautiful patina.

End-Grain Finish

End-grain wood, the result of cuts made perpendicular to the wood grain, takes on a special finish which is clearly visible to the eye. When finish is applied to the ends of cut boards used in furniture construction, these ends will absorb more stain than the surrounding wood and, therefore, appear darker. This is because end grain contains more open tracheid vessels, or pores, with which to absorb the stain.

Although end grain appears in its most obvious form at the end of a cut board, every cut into any board will expose some amount of end grain. All carving, for example, involves end-grain exposure and thus the variation in stain absorption is explained, i.e., rather than dust and dirt collecting in the corners of a typical carving and making it seem darker (although this may be partly true, of course), these cut-in areas are areas of end-grain exposure and consequently have absorbed a larger amount of stain. The claw-and-ball foot is an example of the exposure of end grain. The corners between the claws and the top of the ball are end-grain surfaces and hence will always appear darker, again because of the extra stain absorption due to more tracheid vessels opened with wood cut in this direction (see illustration 40, page 28).

Attempts are made to even the stain between end grain and regular grain by fewer applications to end-grain surfaces or use of a diluted stain on such areas, but total success is almost impossible. Note the variation in color on the photographed cabriole leg. The top side of the pad foot, having greater end-grain exposure, is darker. The

131. Example of smooth closed grain as observed on the bottom of the claw-and-ball foot.

top side of the knee is also darker for the same reason. The turned legs of a Sheraton side chair or early New England slat-back chair owe much of their lovely surface interest to the varied absorption rate of stain, again the intermittent end-grain surfaces absorbing greater quantities and thus appearing darker. End-grain table edges also prove this point.

End grain should not be confused with "open grain." Open grain has a rather strict meaning and is used in reference to old versus new wood. When a piece of mahogany, for example, is freshly cut, the pores (grain) will appear open. In contrast, due to age and applied finish, the grain of an old piece of mahogany will appear closed. Immediately, my grandmother's kitchen table comes to mind. This old table has been rubbed, waxed and even refinished so many times that the grain is totally closed (pores and vessels filled), giving the wood a metallic appearance. This effect must be seen to be truly appreciated. Good examples of smooth closed grain can be found on the bottoms of chair and stool feet, such as the one here shown (see illustration 131).

132. Detail of old gilding. Note hairline cracks and general feeling of age.

In judging the authenticity of an "antique" it is helpful to remember that open-grain wood is rarely found on genuine old pieces. The pores of such pieces have long since been closed up with repeated applications of finish, dirt, wax and the effects of wear.

As mentioned earlier, the grain or pores of some woods are naturally larger than those of others, regardless of age or quantity of applied finish. Ash, oak and walnut are woods with unusually large, open pores. Such pores always mean a "valley and mountain" uneven raw wood surface which requires filling to achieve a smooth surface. During the 18th and 19th centuries, pores of open-grained woods were sometimes filled with "fillers"— scraping varnish, whiting, plaster of paris and glue, to name a few. An ordinary finishing treatment required many coats to conquer the "valleys" of the open grain. As each coat of shellac or varnish filled in some of the valley, the new height added to the "mountain" would be

sanded down. Coats of finish would be applied and treated in this manner until the valley floors were level with the sanded mountain tops, thereby producing a lovely smooth surface.

Gold Leaf Gilding

Gilding with gold (or silver) leaf is a finishing process applied to furniture which dates back to the days of the ancient Egyptian Pharaohs. As early as 3000 B.C., the discovery had been made that the extreme malleability of gold allowed it to be beaten into a skin so thin that it would adhere to a preparation of plaster. In Europe since the Middle Ages, two distinct methods of overlaying wood with gold leaf have been used, oil-gilding and water-gilding.

133. Late 18th-century water-gilded highly styled looking glass (see detail, illustration 132).

gilding is that it can be done on a ground less laborious to prepare.) When water-gilding was planned for a piece, the wood carving was frequently left incomplete, such delicate details as veining being left to the gilder, who cut, layered, and recut them into the gesso ground. Thus, to strip an old looking-glass frame to the bare wood, for example, is to destroy much of the finer detail.

Old gilding simply looks old. All fakery attempts to duplicate this old appearance, and thus all gilding should be studied carefully for appropriate signs. The gilding should show signs of wear and tear, perhaps exposing evidence of old gesso ground. It will contain a number of flecks, checks and marks, often due to loosening gesso ground. The gilded surface will also appear darkened. New flecks and checks are visually very different from those that are old and mellowed, and are thus identifiable. Pictured here is the gilded handrest of a French fauteuil armchair whose badly chipped old gilding reveals the core wood and gesso coating substructure. A test for gold leaf is the use of nitric acid, which will quickly turn green any gold alloy of less than 9 carats. Never clean gilding with water, which will dissolve it, alas another test for true gold leaf; use turpentine for cleaning and a coat of wax for protection.

Lacquer and Japanning

These are two very distinct furniture finishes quite similar in design—the japanning technique in fact having been developed to imitate the true Asian lacquering. Eastern lacquer artisans started with even-grain pine wood which they primed with sticky lacquer. Hemp cloth or silk was then pressed on to form a base. Twenty-four hours later the surface was hard enough to be polished smooth with whetstone, and another coat of lacquer was applied. This lacquer process was repeated twenty to thirty times—with each application carefully brushed on—not too slowly for fear the lacquer would dry too hard and not too quickly lest it not be smooth or hard enough. The *Rhus verniciflua* or "lac tree," whose sap is the basic ingredient of lacquer, is grown only in China, Japan and Malaysia; thus Europeans and Americans were forced to resort to an imitation method in the late 17th century termed "japanning," appropriately suggesting from where came the finest true lacquerware.

In the *Handmaid to The Arts* (1758) the English author Robert Dassie writes that "by japanning is to be understood the art of covering bodies by grounds of opake [sic] colours in varnish; which may be either afterwards decorated by painting or gilding, or left in a plain state." The wood, first treated with a mixture of whitening and size, was then coated with two or more

Oil-gilding. This is a process in which the final application is a preparation of "gold size" (boiled linseed oil) to which the gold adheres. It has the advantage of rendering the gilded surface hard and partly waterproof, but the gold cannot be highly toned or burnished/manipulated (it would scratch or rub off), thus lacking the luster of water-gilding. It is doubtful that the oil-gilding process was ever applied to furniture in the 18th century; a less complex process, and thus cheaper, it was used for outside work such as the gilding of signs and weathervanes. *Water-gilding.* Gilding of this type is always applied on a carefully prepared and smoothed gesso and/or red (etc.) clay (bole) ground applied over the wood, thus to serve as a resilient cushion for the leaf, the gold also reflecting the bole color beneath. (Although a gesso ground is often used for oil-gilding too, one of the advantages of oil-

134. Hand rest of an 18th-century armchair showing core wood and gesso coating under the gilded surface. Visibly layered areas are clarified in the drawing.

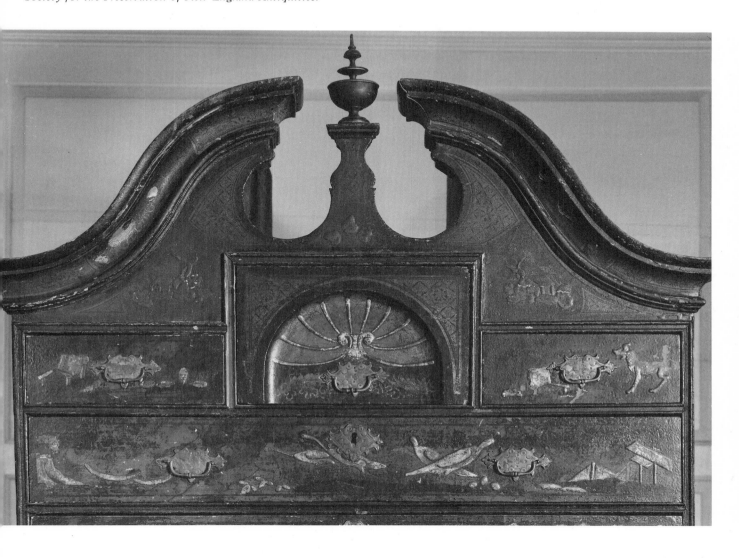

applications of varnish composed of gum-lac, seed-lac or shellac, and dissolved in spirits of wine with other gums and substances also being employed. Black, tortoiseshell and red were the normal base colors. Raised gesso decoration was used on all important pieces. American colonial japanners working in Boston and New York, the two centers for this craft between 1720 and 1750, simplified the English method by using fine-grained woods for their case pieces, thereby eliminating the need for a gesso-like base on the wood surfaces. They also did away with the costly and time-consuming mixing of seed-lac varnish with ground colors by simply applying clear varnish over the coats of paint.

The difference between refined lacquer and japanning techniques becomes obvious when they are compared. Indications of original finish would be the same as those mentioned already for a varnish finish and gilding. Most examples of lacquer have suffered somewhat with age, more so the softer japanned pieces. Scratches, dents, cracks and chips are frequent, as shown in the close-up photo of the original japanned finish on a Boston circa 1745 high chest of drawers (illustration 135). Japanned pieces have also often been coated, probably for protection, with thick opaque varnish which sometimes hides the entire design.

Finish · 91

Dating a Finish

Besides the methods mentioned above, there are additional tests for assessing the age of a finish. One of these is the evidence to be found by removing a drawer pull or other piece of hardware. The "finish" under a pull, although probably cleaner, or different, should nevertheless give an impression consistent with the age of the surrounding wood as in illustration 136. The presence of drip marks may suggest the hasty work of recent finishing, particularly if the drips do not pass the finish tests of age or do not blend or relate to the obvious age of the piece. This is not to say that drip marks made by earlier craftsmen cannot be found, but these drips will react to quick age tests and, more important, will harmonize with their surround.

The use of ultraviolet radiation is an interesting modern technique which is helpful in providing surface finish information. Newly cut, unfinished wood fluoresces very little; the fluorescence of old wood is largely due to the surface patina it has received through the years. Old furniture thus produces some fluorescence due to surface treatment. New varnish, for example, fluoresces a bright violet, while old wood with aged patina fluoresces a whitish color. Although fluorescence alone cannot be used to tell the difference between old and new work, it can reveal additions and alterations more dramatically and effectively than sunlight.

136. *Comparison of surface finish under and around drawer pull. Note how the outline of the brass (encrustation) is absorbed into both areas of finish.*

Chapter 10

Veneer and Marquetry

VENEER

Veneering is a form of joinery and decoration which dates back to ancient Egypt. Veneer work was extensively produced during the 17th, 18th and 19th centuries and still is done to decorate furniture surfaces by using rare and richly figured woods, often combined in patterns. See the delicate, intricate veneer arrangements in the photographed late 18th-century New England card table (illustration 137). Veneering—covering the surface of a comparatively common wood with a thin glued skin of another more exotic and expensive wood—also makes it possible to obtain the greatest use of special rare woods. Wood of a twisty or odd nature (such as walnut burls), which would be too unstable for constructional use in the solid, could be successfully used as thin slices of interesting veneer. As all pieces of a stack of veneers from one piece of wood (known as a flitch or parcel in the trade) are identical, this reality can be exploited by piecing them together in a variety of ways producing matching patterns impossible to obtain with solid wood. (See the matched crotch mahogany-veneered drawer fronts in illustration 8, page 11.) Veneer stringing,

narrow long veneer pieces set into the veneered wood, is often a part of these patterns, and characteristic of 17th-century banded or string veneer work are the different timber veneers on each side of this line of detail. Sometimes when the veneer background is continuous, often a characteristic of late 18th-century pieces, the stringing is a later embellishment.

Furniture cores intended for veneer overlay were usually of fine quality pine (and in England, deal) during the 18th century. (Any core wood imperfection would ultimately effect the surface veneer.) Oak was similarly used, particularly for walnut and the more expensive early mahogany-veneered furniture. After 1750, Honduras mahogany was sometimes used as a ground for veneer. The process of laying down a sheet of veneer required great skill and care on the part of the craftsman. The veneer was applied to the core wood with hot glue, then weighted in place with cauls (or sandbags when the surface curved) and heavy clamping. When the glue became dry the surface was smoothed, planed, sanded and finished.

Before the introduction of machinery, veneer was cut with a handsaw and measured from $1/16''$ to $1/8''$ thick. The thickness of early veneer is apparent in illustration

137. *Late 18th-century New England Federal-style card table of elaborate geometric veneered patterns in contrasting dark and light woods. The curly-figure rectangular front panels are likely to be birch, which is often mistaken for satinwood. Federal-period stringing can be felt, to discover that it is slightly higher than the adjacent veneer, because it was inset as a slight V-shape; with shrinkage movement of veneer, the string inlay moves upward, hence there is projection. (If there is no projection, the string inlay may be modern or the piece has been recently sanded and refinished.)*

138. *Burl walnut-veneered top surface of an early 18th-century dressing table. Burl veneer is characteristically quartered, that is, applied in four sections, as such a large piece of burl would not be obtainable. The veneered burl walnut center is surrounded with herringbone-pattern veneer band inlay and plain-figure walnut cross-banded veneer.*

139. Damaged mahogany veneer surface.

139 which shows a damaged veneer surface on an English mid-18th-century desk-and-bookcase. Now that it is prepared by machinery, veneer is rarely more than 1/32″ thick and often less than 1/60″. This is helpful to know in the detection of fake pieces. It is also one of the reasons why modern veneer holds better than the old hand-cut material, for glue will hold a thin sheet better than a thick one. The unknown varied ingredients contained in historic hide glue also made its holding power unpredictable over time.

In the 19th century a machine was introduced to cut veneers with a knife, slicing it in layers of any thickness required. This remains the modern practice and is carried out in two ways. The first is to slide the log in the same way as saw-cut boards, thus producing "slice veneer" which contains figure similar to that found in old saw-cut veneers. The second is to mount the log in a form of lathe known as a peeler. As the log revolves, a knife is advanced against it, peeling off a continuous band until the whole of the log, except the center, has been cut. This rotary-cut veneer is the width of the trunk's length, thin and absolutely without figure.

There are several other intricacies in veneer cutting which are worthy of note. One of these is the cleaving of burl veneers from the boles of old walnut trees (see page 15). The merchant who trades in fancy veneers is always on the lookout for freak growths, and trees which have been topped/pollarded offer many varieties. Pollarded olive, elm, walnut and ash, for example, yield handsome veneers, although only in small, brittle pieces. As seen in illustration 8, page 11, "crotch mahogany," cut from a tree crotch and split to produce the desirable plume figure, was handsomely exploited by cabinetmakers from the mid-18th century onward. Another refinement was the cutting of saplings and branches transversely into "oyster pieces" (see page 14). Laburnum, with its yellow sap-ring and dark heart, produced handsome examples of this technique, and almond, walnut and kingwood were among the other timbers utilized in this manner.

MARQUETRY

Marquetry is a kind of veneer, a composite of pieces of veneer arranged in elaborate floral patterns and arabesques forming a thin panel which is glued to the core wood. Veneered marquetry was a Dutch craft brought to England in a fully developed state about 1670. It flourished until 1715, especially as ornamentation for tall clock cases, and was again revived by Chippendale and his contemporaries during the late 1760s, using the delicate motifs of the neoclassic style. The laying of

The "arabesque" variety, in wood with a flowing scroll design, was inspired by the brass and tortoiseshell marquetry designs of the French royal cabinetmaker (ébéniste du roi) André-Charles Boulle (1642–1732). Boulle was famous for his method of preparing his decorative marquetry panels: sheets of brass and tortoiseshell were glued together and then cut with a saw to the desired pattern. When cut, the layers were separated and then combined to provide one panel of tortoiseshell ground inlaid with brass and one of brass inlaid with shell, known as "first part" and "counter part." A pair of commodes, therefore, might be veneered, one with first part Boulle marquetry and the other with counter part Boulle work.

In all types of English marquetry the pattern was usually formed by fitting light-colored woods into darker background woods such as walnut, coromandel or lignum vitae. However, French and Continental marquetry represented endless variety in its exquisite design, detail and form. The entire marquetry process was done with a fine saw, thereby providing the scope for elaborate designs. That is to say that the veneers of the design were cut and composed into a panel before the panel was glued to the core—veneer being thin, it could be cut with a saw before application instead of the core wood having to be laboriously chopped away with a chisel to receive the inlay. The many parts to a particular design were each cut separately by the skilled marquetry cutter and they made a perfect fit, one within the other. As the parts were cut they were assembled on a flat tray and paper was glued over the whole to hold it together until final application.

Some marquetry was shaded—especially the green stained holly wood leaves of flowers. This was done by dipping one end of the piece (or leaf) of veneer into hot sand so that it became slightly scorched. The inlaid light wood urns on the legs of the drop-leaf table (illustration 162, page 114) have sand-scorched details. Such shading was permanent and could be controlled by the amount of time the wood was immersed and the extent of veneer covered by the sand. The veins of leaves or the petals of a flower, when made of one piece of veneer, were produced by saw cuts which were then filled with dark colored wax to accentuate them. Much of this subtle detail is lost when the piece is refinished—an indication, incidentally, that the piece *has* been refinished.

Parquetry

Parquetry is a variation of the marquetry veneer technique, contemporary with the late 17th-century marquetry fashion, in which the veneer pieces of wood were fitted together in repeating geometric patterns. An English Carolean-style cabinet-on-stand, circa 1685,

140. *French fall-front secrétaire, veneered marquetry with bronze doré mounts, made by Jean-Henri Riesener (1734–1806) for Queen Marie Antoinette in 1790. Riesener's signature appears at the bottom right of the lower marquetry panel. Photograph courtesy The Frick Collection.*

veneers in scrolls and foliated patterns worked in brass and ebonized wood again came into favor in the Regency period of the early 1800s. Marquetry was also introduced into France from Holland, again in the late 17th century, where it never lost interest or appeal, especially in the urbane court circle of Paris during the 18th century.

The design of early marquetry copied from the Dutch was floral, depicting flowers in vases with birds and utilizing many woods. The "seaweed" variety of marquetry has a pattern representing flowing lines of seaweed and involved only one wood to contrast with the ground; it also resembles the finer leaves of the endive plant and thus is occasionally described as "endive marquetry."

with veneered oysterpieces and cross-cuttings of geometric diamonds made of contrasting walnut veneer would be an example of this type of decorative work.

The most elaborate examples of parquetry veneer are to be found on 18th-century French pieces. Not only have subtle variations of color been echoed back and forth by geometric diaper (repeating) pattern parquetry but on finer pieces stylized floral designs were inlaid against the parquetry ground. This detail work is pointed up and framed (thus protected) with bronze doré mounts and moldings held in place with screws. Close examination of such superbly veneered pieces of furniture should always reveal carefully chosen, matched veneers and finely drawn and cut marquetry parts. It should be remembered that the Paris and provincial guilds of marqueteurs demanded a high standard of craftsmanship from their members, and that a master ébéniste would not permit any work to leave his shop which did not come up to these standards. Thus any piece exhibiting poorly done marquetry work becomes highly suspect.

141. Detail of the fall-front center panel of the Riesener secrétaire, showing the varieties of wood used in the marquetry work and the richly sculptured bronze doré mounts. Photograph courtesy The Frick Collection.

Part **II**

WHAT HAPPENS TO FURNITURE WITH TIME

Chapter 11

Points of Wear

WEAR, SUCH A UNIVERSAL happening caused by time and use, plays an informative role in the analysis of potentially old and therefore "antique" furniture. It will be realized, as we explore the many things that happen to furniture over time, that wear is only one consideration. However, it becomes a most obvious and readily identifiable factor once serious searching begins. Signs of wear serve as good evidence that the piece has been used for a long time, thus quite naturally having marks of wear. This is certainly some proof that the piece is old.

The search for signs of wear is a matter of common sense, since wear will be the result of how and where the piece of furniture is or was used. Wear will not be evenly located everywhere on a piece; every "moveable" (piece of furniture) has some parts which are subject to particular stress and others which receive frequent handling. These areas will show the greatest signs of wear.

TABLES AND CHAIRS

Many signs and degrees of wear can be observed in studying a table. These will vary according to the purpose and use of the table but will be there. Signs to look for include an uneven table top surface, smoothed and/or irregular edges, and scratches. The corners on an old table are likely to be nicked and bruised where chairs have knocked against them. If the table has a trestle base, this will no doubt show the wearing down and markings of many shoes having rested there in the past. Table legs and feet too, will show signs of use from being marred by chairs and cleaning implements, as well as being used as resting spots for shoes. Sometimes the feet of a table will be almost entirely worn away. This is often true for early examples of butterfly, gateleg and tavern tables with their small turned button or knob feet.

An old chair is also likely to have many points of wear. The first point might be at the top of the back, where a hand has probably clutched the chair untold times to bring it to the table. Consequently, the top rail will be smooth and worn. Again, the back is likely to show signs of having been pushed up against the wall, and of people leaning it against the wall while sitting on it. Proof of this habit is often evidenced by the uneven wear on the wall-side of banister-back chair finials (see illustration 143). This finial wear is especially evident on chairs with backward-raked stiles, such as tall William and Mary–style chairs.

Because chairs are frequently dragged from area to area in the line of use, the legs over time will show many signs of abuse and wear. (See illustration 124, page 81.)

142. *Five-banister-back New England armchair, circa 1700–1720.*

143. *Backs of the ball-and-button finials on banister-back chair showing extensive wear from use.*

144. *Period Queen Anne–style pad foot with usual signs of use and wear.*

145. *Detail of chair stretcher showing signs of genuine wear.*

146. *Turned front stretchers on a child's high chair well-worn by children's feet.*

Typically, the outer sides of the front and back legs (or feet if the chair has them) will be bruised and sometimes smoothed or even partially worn away. (See illustration 130, page 86.) In some cases, the feet will have completely disappeared. The bottom of feet, when closely studied, will appear to have a hard polish scored by fine lines where, over time, particles of grit have been trapped between the wood and the floor surface. (See the bottom of the claw-and-ball foot, illustration 131, page 87.) Edge wear can sometimes be confirmed by tilting and dragging an old chair and comparing where the wear should appropriately be and where in fact it is.

Among the most charming points of wear on a chair are the uneven stretchers. These will often be partially worn (and thus uneven) from use as resting spots for shoes. The wear will be found to be deeper on the outside than on the inside edge of the stretcher, and the line of wear will tend to be fairly regular, as the foot did not always rest in exactly the same spot. On a spurious piece, however, the appearance of wear will usually be quite uneven and wear marks will be as deep on the inside of the stretcher as on the outside.

Chair arms and handholds will sometimes show similar signs of wear. Note the detail photograph of a "carver" chair (illustration 147). Child versions of these

147. *Massachusetts, Plymouth-area oak "carver" chair, circa 1665–1680, with worn ball turned handhold and wear on the turned arm.*

148. *Old mahogany drawer front. Note the dents and bruises on the cock-bead or continuous-bead molding.*

149. *Signs of wear on oak drawer front, Boston chest of drawers, circa 1690–1710.*

Pilgrim-type chairs will often reveal that the back sides of the backposts have been worn flat from top to foot. The reason might seem mysterious until one lays the chair on its back on the floor. The whole backpost rests flatly on the floor and the upturned chair seat is just the right height for a toddling one-year-old child. A good guess might consequently be that such a chair was used as a "walker," and this wear on the chair posts is due to the child pushing the chair about on the floor. The banister-back chair in illustration 143 shows wear on its posts, along with the finials, suggesting that it, too, has been used as a walker.

CASE PIECES

With case pieces many of the same points of wear and use are in evidence. Bracket or claw-and-ball feet of a chest of drawers or a desk-and-bookcase, for example, will show signs of wear from being knocked against; part of a foot may be worn or broken away from being moved or dragged about; and any number of bangs, dents, marks and stains will be noticeable everywhere. Old clock cases are frequently damaged to some extent at their base by brooms and other objects and by the impact of feet during winding. Although this latter point of wear is rarely noticed, observation will bear it out. With some clock cases, a protective strip of wood, appropriately called a kick-plate, is added to the bottom of the case.

The drawers of a case piece are an excellent source for signs of wear. The front of the drawer will show the signs of use one might well expect—the edges are apt to be uneven, bruised and marked from the drawer being opened and shut, sometimes not so gently (see illustration 148). The primary surface is also likely to show occasional scratches and blemishes from use. Small indentations and scratches will be especially noticeable under the keyholes of slant-front desks, the upper doors of desk-and-bookcases and drawers, due to other keys on the bunch knocking against the surface below as former owners worked the locks. Note the wear marks caused by the photographed 17th-century pull dropping and swinging into place after use (see illustration 149).

The underside of the drawer, especially the runners, is an area of great wear in a case piece. Each time the drawer is opened and closed, the runners and their tracks are utilized; in even a short time signs of use and some wear will be obvious. On an 18th-century chest of drawers for example, evidence of wear should be extreme, even allowing for the cabinetmaker's precautionary use of reinforced hardwoods for the runners and their tracks. With careful investigation of all the drawers in a desk, one might discover that some of the runners or their tracks have been replaced. (Even the replacements may show signs of wear.) See and compare illustrations 181 and 182 on pages 126 and 127 with this in mind. Although these replacements may detract from the 100% originality of the piece, the fact that they have been necessary certainly indicates wear and use over time.

150. Seventeenth-century English Carolean chair crest rail. The cupid is quite flattened with wear, as is the flower under the crown.

151. Clarification of carving wear on chair crest rail.

CARVING

Carving is a very important point of wear. All carving on a piece should be examined carefully. The bits of carving that project farthest may be slightly rounded, smoothed and damaged from contact and exposure. A case in point is the carving on the back of a Carolean chair which has been rubbed smooth over the years because people have sat back against it. Other projecting areas of carving, always the most vulnerable, may well have been nicked or broken off. (Rococo Chippendale looking glasses and picture frames are such examples.) Despite the natural mishaps suffered by carved areas over time, those areas of shallow carving and thus of lower relief may remain very crisp, clear and intact. This is because the higher relief carving has served as protection (see illustration 151).

Chapter 12

Shrinkage

SHRINKAGE

THE IMPORTANT TERM SHRINKAGE is here defined as the natural reduction of the moisture content causing contraction in a piece of wood found in its final form—as a part of a piece of furniture. Wood is constantly expanding and contracting slightly as its moisture content reacts to an increase or decrease of moisture in the atmosphere; this is the hygroscopic quality of wood. When a tree is felled in the forest, it contains more moisture than it ever will again—over 50%. (Because of this moisture, it will also weigh its greatest amount.) It is thus necessary that some drying ("seasoning") take place before a newly cut log is worked any further, thereby naturally reducing and stabilizing the moisture content to some degree. The traditional method, air drying, was to stack the "green" logs on racks outdoors under a shelter and let the air run its natural course of evaporation over a year or two of time. The kiln method of drying wood is more often used today because it accomplishes the task very quickly—the green newly cut wood is placed in a kiln and "seasoned" via slow heat.

Seasoned wood, with its relatively stabilized moisture content, its consequential increased stability and strength in use, and its greater resistance to decay, still reacts to some extent to changes in the atmospheric humidity. Finished wood, despite this extra protection, is also subject to gradual movement.

Because shrinkage or contraction is a natural and inevitable action of all wood, old furniture made of wood will likely display some signs of shrinkage. Such signs include protruding pegs, loose panels in Wainscot chairs, loose creaking joints due to tenon shrinkage and spaces between cabinet doors. It should be kept in mind that signs of shrinkage are rare with falsified pieces, owing to their cores having been made from old material which has already shrunk before being used the second time.

The cyclical nature of shrinkage is demonstrated by the expansion and contraction that occurs yearly on the English late 17th-century solid oak clock-case door pictured here (illustrations 153 and 154). In the first of these photographs, taken during a Boston warm humid summer, the door measures its intended width—it covers the opening, and the parts of the lock catch and work

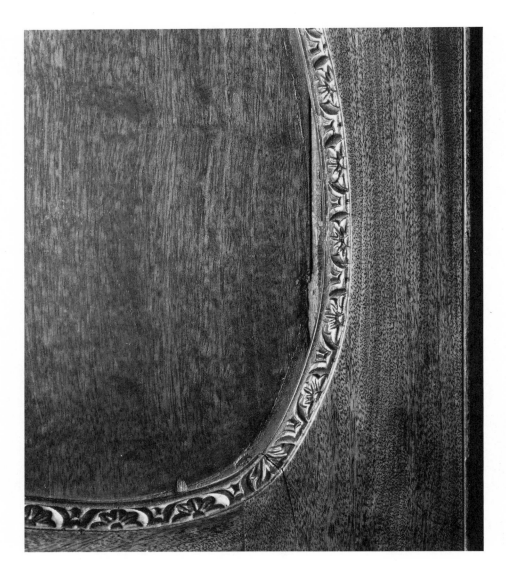

152. *The panel of an 18th-century desk-and-bookcase upper case door. Note how shrinkage has exposed some of its chamfered edge, meant to fit into the frame grooving. Lower on the panel it has cracked as the shrinking power has pulled the panel free from its frame, which must have been holding it securely.*

properly. However, in mid-January, with dry central heating conquering the 10-degree (Fahrenheit) Boston winter, great shrinkage takes place: the door has so shrunk across the grain (its width) as to cause a space between the door and the case framing and sometimes the lock is sufficiently displaced so that it no longer catches. The degree of shrinkage involved here has been dramatized in illustration 154 by placing a light in the interior of the case while the photograph was being taken.

As noted earlier, wood grain runs up and down the log (review the log drawings, illustration 10, page 12). When a log is cut into boards for use in furniture construction, the grain of each board and its direction can be determined. Even in a finished piece of furniture, the grain direction can be easily identified (see, for example, illustration 152). Once this identification has been made, it is possible to determine how wood will move according to the principle of wood shrinkage: *all wood shrinks across the grain*. Hence a board, with time, will shrink both in width and thickness (across the grain) but not in length, which is in the direction of the grain.* This double aspect of shrinkage is called "differential shrinkage." In considering the nature of shrinkage, it may be helpful to think of the common sponge—as the water evaporates, the sponge shrinks.

*Contraction is much greater—and often uneven (thus warping)—with plain-sawed boards (i.e., sawed tangentially to the growth rings) than with those which have been radially cut (see illustration 21, page 16). (Quarter-sawed timber is obtained from a log which has been cut into four horizontal sections or quarters; each section is then radially sawed into boards or veneer, although some cuts will vary from a true radial path.) Contraction also occurs more readily in lateral directions than along the axis of growth, where shrinking is minute. This is because the sapwood of a tree has a higher moisture content than the heartwood, and when timber is sawn into planks, the distribution of moisture in the planks varies accordingly.

153. *Seventeenth-century oak clock-case door with normal intended width.*

154. *Seventeenth-century oak clock-case door after shrinkage.*

155. *Shrinkage movement is always across the grain.*

Shrinkage · 109

156. Example of breadboard shrinkage.

33½"

33"

157. Effect of shrinkage on round tea table.

158. *Calliper measurement of old wood, showing the baluster section to measure oval in the direction of the wood grain.*

159. *Calliper measurement of new wood, showing the baluster section to measure round, a calliper measurement proving the same when taken across the grain and with the grain. Thus, this is a new turned baluster with no shrinkage yet having taken place.*

 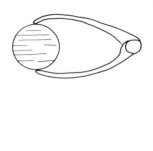

EXAMPLES OF SHRINKAGE MOVEMENT

So-called "breadboard" ends to tables and slant-front desks will always show signs of shrinkage, however slight. Illustration 156 is a close-up detail of a corner of the slant front on an 18th-century Boston-area mahogany slant-front desk. Because the grain of the ends (breadboards) of the hinged slant front are perpendicular to the main horizontal board, whose grain runs horizontally, the large horizontal board has shrunk, as can be seen by examining the join of the horizontal and vertical boards.

Wood shrinkage is also evident upon close examination of a "round" pie-crust mahogany tea table. Upon measurement of perpendicular diameters on the table top, it will be realized that, in fact, the table is oval. This is so because the wood has shrunk across the grain and, consequently, the table is longer in the direction in which the grain runs.

Round turned legs, whether one of the heavy oak legs of a late 17th-century table or a smooth, simple, turned late 18th-century Sheraton-style leg, speak to the same principle. Because wood shrinks across the grain and the wood grain runs vertically with the legs, any and all old legs will thus measure oval when measured with a calliper in two directions. Illustrations 158 and 159 show how the calliper is used to prove this inevitable truth.

Shrinkage is also the cause of cracks in the sides of case pieces. The cracks shown in the highboy pictured in illustration 160 are in the direction of the wood grain—vertical in the upper case and horizontal in the lower case. Once again wood shrinkage across the grain has caused cracking, all edges of this single-board side being held firmly to the frame of the highboy; thus the weakest area is its middle. As natural shrinkage takes place, the board gives way at the weakest point, causing the crack. (As we have seen, the same principle applies to the tea table top, illustration 77, page 49.)

If more than one board was used on the side of a highboy or table top, the individual boards would often shrink across the grain and eventually pull apart, leaving spaces between them. Illustration 93, page 63, shows the

160. Eighteenth-century highboy (high chest of drawers)
with shrinkage cracks typical of case pieces.

top and back of an English mid-Georgian chest of drawers where several boards have been simply and crudely nailed to the carcase frame. These boards have split and spaced with shrinkage, and the cabinetmaker has subsequently covered the spaces with tape—a common practice.

Shrinkage is often seen in the bottom of drawers. As several boards have been used, natural shrinkage has resulted in spaces between these boards today; i.e., each board has shrunken across the grain and hence reduced slightly in width, thereby creating empty spaces. (Review drawer drawings, illustrations 64–68, pages 42–43.)

Again we identify shrinkage movement and its exploitation in an analysis of cornerblocks. Because the wood grain of the cornerblock runs in a direction contrary to the wood grain of the member it supports (see illustration 42, page 30), its shrinkage movement counterbalances the shrinkage movement of the member and thus serves its function of support to the member. This movement will, in time, cause the glue holding the block to give way (sometimes cornerblocks are also nailed or screwed into position), although the block may remain held at one end almost indefinitely provided it does not get a knock to sever the small remaining glue area. (Photographed cornerblocks can be seen in illustrations 233 and 234, page 165.) Incidentally, due to the reduced size of the cornerblock caused by shrinkage, many come loose, fall out and get lost. Therefore, one is likely to find cornerblocks missing on the underside of a chair, etc., or later inconsistent replacements.

Illustration 161 shows a handsome oval-shaped late 18th-century Massachusetts wine cooler with the usual

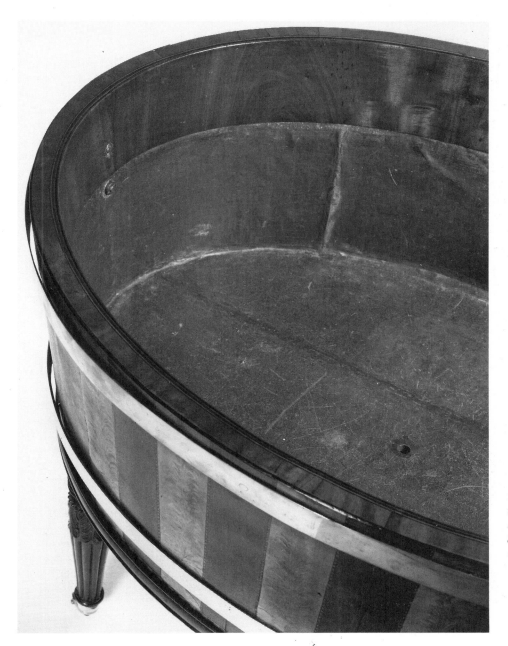

161. Mahogany-and-satinwood-veneered wine cooler, circa 1795, attributed to cabinetmaker John Seymour of Boston. Note loose banding due to shrinkage.

162. Detail of Federal-style Baltimore mahogany drop-leaf table, 1795–1810, showing "spread-eagling." (Note the elegant characteristic Baltimore bellflower pictorial inlay, of elongated proportions and made of three, sometimes five, separate shaded parts.)

The "spread-eagled" so-called Pembroke drop-leaf table shown (illustration 162) illustrates an unfortunate result of shrinkage. "Spread-eagling" refers to the small leaves of these tables which can no longer hang straight down, thereby suggesting the spread wings of an eagle. Since these table leaves are made in keeping with the wood-grain direction of their tops, when they shrink (across the grain), the leaves are drawn in until they touch the underframe when they are down, and eventually they will no longer hang vertically. This is because the leaves and top have become smaller than the frame on which they rest due to shrinkage. In extreme cases, the tension is finally released by the top splitting in half.

Another example of natural wood shrinkage is found in the mitre-joined corners of picture frames or the door moldings in an old house. For seemingly no apparent reason the parts have pulled apart, leaving a gap. In fact, the wood has shrunk across the grain, thereby creating a space between the two sections (see illustrations 163 and 164).

Cracking of veneer or panels of wardrobes, sides of bookcases and cabinets, and tops of drop-leaf tables, particularly during the early 18th century when much walnut veneer was used and again during the late 18th century with the use of satinwood and other exotic veneer, is the result of shrinkage. These surface cracks in the veneer are caused by the shrinking of the core wood onto which the veneers are glued. As the core shrinks, such movement being inevitable, the top surface reacts by cracking (or moving). To further complicate matters, the direction of the core wood grain was usually perpendicular to that of the veneered surface. Thus, as the core shrinkage took place, the veneer sometimes buckled. A typical example is the late 18th-century mahogany-veneered tall clock by Jno Kent of Manchester, England, detail shown here (illustration 166). Illustration 165 shows how the different directions of the two woods moving with natural shrinkage in time will cause the weaker, the veneer, to give way with cracks and buckles—or worse. The veneers themselves are unlikely to shrink to any proportionate degree because they have been cut so thin (about 1/16″ on 18th-century furniture) as to have inadequate power. When inlay stringing as part of the veneer surface is also involved (as in this clock-case example), it will also react to core movement by buckling and looping up with its excess, as in illustration 189, page 131. (In general, the edges of 18th-century inlay stringing can be felt because the veneers on either side have shrunk slightly away from the stringing.)

Warping is an unpredictable and most unhappy kind of shrinkage. By definition, a warped board is as it is because of irregularities in the rate or direction of shrinkage, most frequently caused by the uneven reaction to changes of moisture content in the surrounding air relative to changes in the temperature, the so-called

lead lining. Alternating panels of dark and light wood have been veneered onto the core wood and further decoration and support is provided by wide brass bandings. As one looks down on this cooler today, some 170 years later, one discovers large spaces between the banding and the veneer surface. Shrinkage has reduced the size of the entire piece. (Notice how it is also possible to sight down the reeded leg.)

163. Mitre-joined corner pulled apart by cross-grain shrinkage.

164. Japanned looking glass with mitre corner shrinkage.

165. Effects of natural core shrinkage movement on veneer.

166. Eighteenth-century tall-clock case with cracking, buckling and veneer-loosening problems.

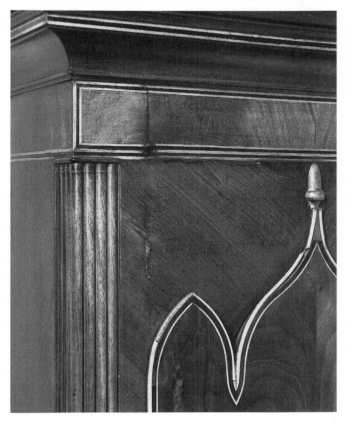

167. *Warpage (and buckling) involves irregular wood movement beyond the normal cross-grain shrinkage; the top of this drawn gateleg table exaggerates such movement to better identify it.*

168. *Warpage in the form of dishing can be recognized as part of the character of this American late 17th-century gateleg table. Most warps are permanent and can be removed only by applying severe stresses, with potential damage to the wood. (Note the deep and crisp turning of the baluster-turned legs.)*

169. *Windsor chair with details showing evidence of shrinkage. Note the leg protruding through the shield-shape thick plank seat (a shape unique to Windsor side chairs) and back spindle extending beyond the top of the bow. Photographs courtesy The Society for the Preservation of New England Antiquities.*

"RH" factor. The tendency toward warp or distortion is always present, for shrinkage is not entirely uniform throughout any species of wood, especially in woods of uneven density or where there are defects in a board. Those woods with a straight grain and uniform texture are less prone to warping than those with interlocked, cross or spiral grains, as all these tend to shrink unevenly. Warpage (and buckling) involving this irregular wood movement beyond the normal cross-grain shrinkage usually creates havoc when it appears. It may be in the form of dishing—concave shrinkage across the grain—or in the form of twisting, spiral shrinkage. Great character comes with the warping and shrinking of the gateleg table seen in illustrations 167 and 168.

A wonderful lesson in shrinkage is had with the study of the American late 18th-century Windsor chair (see illustration 169). Here the cabinetmaker has exploited his knowledge of how and why woods shrink to produce a very sound, yet attractive chair. In addition to using a selection of woods, such as pine for the seat because it is relatively soft and easily worked for scooping to body contours, maple or birch as legs and stretchers for their strength to withstand stress and strain, and hickory for bows because of its bending ability, the parts were assembled from green wood. This green wood was used so that the green pieces in drying would shrink tightly together, making inseparable joints and stronger chairs. Therefore, legs would thus shrink (always across the grain) around the stretchers. The seat would thus shrink around the legs and back spindles. (In fact, as in illustration 169, one sometimes sees where the legs have protruded right up through the chair seat due to the differential shrinkage of the seat; i.e., shrinkage has taken place across the grain on two surfaces—the seat top and its side—thus reducing the size of the seat on two planes.) Furthermore, the baluster-turned leg has become slightly oval due to its own cross-grain shrinkage. The arms and bow, too, have shrunk tightly around the spindles. Again the green-wood bow shrinkage is apparent in illustration 169, as the wedged tenon of the back spindle, also slightly elongated, extends through and beyond the top of the bow.

Chapter 13

Repairs and Restoration

OLD FURNITURE OFTEN SHOWS signs of repairs and restoration that have required varying degrees of skill plus considerable time, patience and ingenuity. The essence of a good repair is that it should be invisible or as nearly so as possible. Such a result can rarely be accomplished quickly or by a craftsman who does not take pride in his work.

Repairs can be classified under two headings: repairs intended to make an object strong and serviceable again (structural repairs) and repairs intended to preserve an object for posterity's eye—sometimes referred to as cosmetic repairs. Restoration can be defined as a repair which involves the insertion of a new part; like repair, it can be intended either to make a piece useable again or to return it to its original appearance. Bear in mind, however, that 100% restoration results in a reproduction.

REASONS FOR REPAIR

It is difficult to lay down general rules as to when or where a repair or restoration is justified. This will depend on the individual case and is frequently a matter of common sense. A first consideration might be the importance of stopping further damage from taking place. A second would be the need to restore an object to its full use. When repair is decided upon, care should be taken to proceed in a way that will not mar a piece's overall appearance. Thus, if new parts (which should be accurate replicas based on surviving counterpart elements or historic documentation) are to be inserted, they will need to be given an appearance of age and wear so as to match their surround; in fact, how well this is done determines a good restoration. The new wood graft should also be consistent with the old in kind, color, grain and finish. If one chair out of a set of chairs, for example, requires a new front stretcher and all of the other chairs have worn stretchers, it would seem appropriate to make the restoration as invisible as possible by treating the new stretcher of the same wood species and matched color with a spokeshave, chisel and sandpaper to produce the effects of wear.

Museum furniture conservation (with a Code of Ethics established by the American Institute for Conservation of Historic and Artistic Works [AIC] in the late 1960s), unlike traditional repair and restoration, is concerned with the stability of the object (implying no further use or wear) and the preservation of its historic integrity (original materials and workmanship). Thus, repairs are

118

170. *Replacement hinge for hinged lid of slant-front desk (view of writing interior). The hinge is a suitably old one of wrought iron with old screws but its size has necessitated surface patches.*

171. *"White wood" repair on the back-side crest rail of a Chippendale-style chair which is part of an historic house museum collection.*

left in plain view to identify them as such, and stability repairs are minimized. (A conservator always prepares a treatment report listing specific materials and processes used.) Admittedly, many pieces in museums have had later additions which have been "antiqued" (made to blend with their surround). They may also have had repairs and restoration which have become old and worn in themselves as a consequence of subsequent usage before the pieces found their way into the museum. Photography is very helpful in the investigation of repairs, since the surface of a repair in a large photograph will appear different from the surrounding wood.

There are occasions when an owner may decide to "retire" a piece of furniture in weak or faulty condition in order to preserve its remaining originality. For example, the old rush seat on a slat-back chair, though weak and tattered and unsafe for use, may be retained and the chair withdrawn from use for the sake of conserving the old rush. Broken structural parts should always be made good, however, and that as soon as possible after breakage. Missing moldings should be replaced and a badly smashed corner needs attention. A surface finish, however, should never be stripped unless it is in such bad condition that there is no alternative. To clean off the patina of years so as to rid the surface of a few scratches and markings is pure vandalism. Fortunately, the high cost of repairs and restoration influences moderation in this matter. The more valuable a piece, the more conservative will be the attitude of the owner, curator and conservator about its treatment.

Whatever the defect, the necessary repair should be done as quickly as possible, because the failure of one part often throws extra strain on others so that these, in turn, begin to suffer. Thus, a chair leg which has become loose involves movement in adjoining parts—causing other joints to loosen. Broken-off parts have a habit of disappearing, and it is thus wise to refix them while they

are still present. When parts are first broken, the edges are sharp and clean and they can be put back in the most unnoticeable way. When left off for any length of time, the corners of these broken pieces become rounded or otherwise changed and a really clean join becomes impossible. Then, too, cleaning and handling results in furniture cream or grease finding its way to the newly exposed surfaces which are to be glued; all of this has to be removed if the glue is to do its work properly.

Perhaps the biggest problem is that of replacing parts when there is no means of knowing what the originals

172. *Brewster-type "great chair" from the Massachusetts Plymouth area, 1640–1660, of maple and ash. Spindles beneath the arm include two 19th-century replacement spindles and two inverted original spindles. The ball handholds on the front posts are also replacements.*

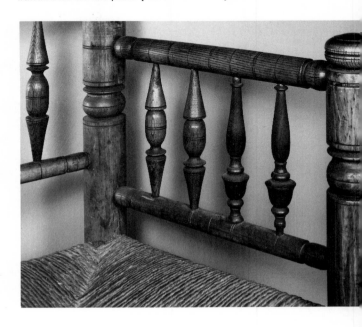

were like. Whenever possible, the new component should be matched to an old one, otherwise the repairer will have to rely on his knowledge of period styles and his eye for balance and scale.

A repair should not lower the value of an article. Given the condition of a chair as needing repair, its value should increase if the repairs are made invisible and structurally sound. This seems straightforward but many "repairers" do not behave accordingly. They undertake a repair too difficult for them, thereby often destroying the piece, or they make repairs which are not reversible, i.e., cannot be undone, despite improved materials and greater craftsman skills in the future. Diverted saw-edge fasteners, more commonly called "corrugated dogs," for example, are sometimes useful strengthening devices, provided they are hammered in straight and not bent over and if they are used in comparatively heavy timbers. Put in badly, or in thin or small timber sections, they are potential instruments of destruction. Using nails, like-wise, despite their indispensability in woodworking, should seldom be part of the wood repairer's activity. It is often necessary to repair additional damage to already damaged woodwork caused by the misguided use or overuse of nails. Even screws, when used too near a fracture, or in too delicate or weak a part, or too long or in too heavy a gauge, can add to the destruction. The number-one repairing tool for the woodworker is glue!

All complicated repair and restoration work should be placed in the hands of an experienced and knowledgeable craftsman. This is especially true for furniture of importance, in terms of age, design and tradition. The intent of this chapter is not to provide a "how to" manual for repairs. However, a few comments on the main categories of repair and restoration may be helpful to the reader as a guide to the problems inherent in old furniture which may, ultimately, require repair or restoration work.

173. *Good repair of back leg and veneer damage on this circa 1825 Empire-style chair.*

174. *Bad repair of joint of back leg with seat rail, and of damaged veneer on this American Empire–style mahogany side chair.*

THE REPARATION OF CHAIRS

There is probably a greater variety of problems in chair repairs than in any other piece of furniture. This is largely because of the many forms a chair takes, and because a chair is subjected to more strain and has to put up with more abuse than any other kind of furniture. In normal use it must take the weight of a person and frequently must withstand the strain of being leaned back upon by the sitter and even being tilted onto its back legs. Other stresses are applied when a chair is knocked over backwards or comes into contact with obstacles while being carried.

Faults may vary from a simple local fracture or the breakage of an arm or leg, to the loosening of some or all of the joints. When only a single joint or pair of joints has given way, it is often possible to put things right by regluing without disassembling the entire piece. An experienced cabinetmaker tries to avoid taking the whole chair apart unless all the joints are loose, since further damage could easily be caused. A general rule in fact is to always do the minimum, for in attempting the maximum repair it is easy to make things worse.

Again, because of the many stresses and demands put upon a chair, all of its parts are vulnerable. For the sake of design, many of these parts are highly impractical for their purpose—for example, the pierced and carved shield-shaped back of a Hepplewhite-style side chair. Illustration 176 pictures a Chippendale-style chair back with damage on the crest rail and on some areas of the splat. The inherent weakness in this delicate back prevents it from standing up to much wear and strain, even if it is in good condition.

175. English Regency chair, with detail showing crack in the back stile caused by leverage placed on the chair back.

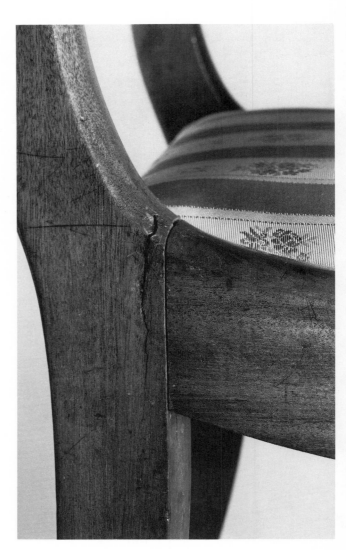

THE REPARATION OF TABLES

The chief troubles that occur with table tops are those of warping, broken joints and splits. Warped table tops have always been a problem for which there is no totally satisfactory solution. As noted in Chapter 12, warpage is especially likely to occur when the wood grain is of an unusually twisty character. Often the warpage is in the form of the top's edges curling upward—probably because wood tends to curl toward the light. As a rule, too, the top surface is polished and so sealed, whereas the underside surface is left bare, allowing moisture from the air to enter beneath and so swell the grain.

Attempts have often been made to counteract warpage by dampening the concave area and reversing the top for a few hours. This is of little use, for the table top resumes its curved shape as it dries out. The moisture will scarcely penetrate the polish, and it is likely to mark the surface instead.

When a warped table top is fixed to a rigid underframe and is not too thick, it is sometimes possible to clamp it down and screw afresh, thus holding it in a flat position. This however is done on the assumption that the false top or top rails of the understructure are firmly in position—otherwise, the curved and warped top will lift them.

When the table is of no special value, a simple though drastic cure is to cut the top into strips, plane the edges to give a flat surface, and glue up afresh. An extra piece is inserted to allow for the waste in sawdust and shavings. This, of course, cannot be done when the top is polished or of finely figured wood, since it would destroy both the polish and the figure. An alternative and almost as dramatic a cure would be to make a series of cuts along the length on the underside about ⅔ of the thickness of the wood in depth, clamp flat and glue in strips of the same kind of wood where necessary.

The above method is effective if properly done, but calls for careful consideration. If the cuts are too deep, the wood is liable to show a series of flats, this being especially marked if the cuts are wide apart. If the spacing is too wide, the local bending becomes obvious; when the cuts are closer together there is less local bending in each, since the total bend is spread over a greater number.

When joints have failed, the only plan is to "shoot" the joint anew with glue. If care is taken, it is possible to avoid the planing of the surface afterwards, always an important advantage when the table top is polished.

Splits along the grain of the wood, as distinct from failed joints, require an entirely different treatment. It is useless to rub in glue and clamp together unless the split is very slight—it will invariably open again because the wood is under considerable stress. One satisfactory

176. *Damaged and partially repaired Chippendale-style chair back.*

177. *Grooving for the correction of a warped table top.*

solution is to open the split slightly, clean out any old polish or wax and lay in a strip of wood which matches the grain of the old as closely as possible. Another successful treatment is a supporting wood insert, butterfly-shaped to hold the two sides of the split together. This is called a dovetail key. An example of this is seen on the underside of the Chippendale-style tilt-top tea table shown here.

THE REPARATION OF CASE PIECES

Case furniture—since it involves mechanical moving parts (especially drawers)—inevitably shows signs of usage and thus need of repair. Friction takes its toll, and the strain of a drawer constantly being pulled open involves considerable wear, particularly when the drawer is laden beyond its capacity (and most drawers usually are). However, no one expects or wishes drawers to have sharp edges and perfect fitting after 100 years or more of active service. (An example of wear on the drawer of a desk-and-bookcase is seen in illustration 148, page 104.)

Problems typical of drawers include broken or loose joints, worn sides, broken and shrunken drawer bottoms and worn runners. When the corner joints of a drawer are loose, there is only one thing for the cabinetmaker to do—separate and reglue the parts. Worn drawer runners

are always a problem. When it is possible to remove and replace them (or remove and reverse them), this is often an advantage, though it is still necessary to make good the wear across the front rail. Sometimes it is impossible, or awkward, to remove the runners, or there may be a solid piece from front to back rather like a shelf, and it becomes necessary to make good the deeply worn troughs.

Another variety of repair requiring yet further skills on the part of the cabinetmaker is that involved with the lathe. Candlesticks, turned legs and turned spindles all spun on the lathe, may require total replacements. In the case of the typical old turned leg of a Windsor chair, now oval from cross-grain shrinkage with time, the new part, after turning, must be carved down to oval measurement, to match the original. A break in a chair spindle may sometimes involve grafting, replacing a section of the spindle with the new wood. The necessary amount and size will dictate the required new turning; when ready, the new section can be whittled to the old or dowelled together. Hide glue should always be used on such occasions rather than white glue, which, as was noted earlier, is so strong that the parts are unlikely to separate should later repairs make this necessary.

An alternative method of repair, when it is desirable to use as much of the old spindle as possible, is to run a metal rod up through the spindle, thus holding together and strengthening the parts. A lathe would be used to bore the hole up through the old spindle. This is a very intricate repair and requires the experience and skill of an accomplished cabinetmaker for successful results.

179. *Dovetail-key repair.*

180. *Drawer bottom repair of inserted new wood, necessitated by cross-grain shrinkage.*

Fitting is an initial and important consideration in much repair work. Broken parts should be fitted together dry before the addition of glue, to determine damage, missing bits and how best to repair. Chairs and table frames should always be fitted square and then glued and clamped up dry. However, if old marks indicate the original fitting to have been made uneven and off-square, the new fitting should return parts to the original spots. Likewise, if a piece has become warped or uneven causing off-square measurements, new fittings of broken parts should not attempt to change this state of affairs.

THE REPARATION OF VENEER

Almost all furniture made from veneer sections glued to core timber, unless correctly built and carefully maintained, will eventually need restoration or some form of surface repair. In addition to accidental damage, extremes in climatic conditions (especially when pieces of furniture are moved to warmer climates) and the drying effects of central heating often aggravate damage.

Veneer is particularly prone to three kinds of damage. The first of these is the superficial damage to the polished surface caused by wear and tear. This can usually be repaired by polishing procedures. The second is the damage which occurs to decorative veneers, inlays, bandings and ornaments, often resulting from loss of adhesion at the glue line. The third kind of damage that affects veneered old furniture (this type is both the most common and the most serious) results from movement in the core wood, which may have either swollen or shrunken, causing twisting, warping or splitting of the surface veneer. (An example of clock-case movement can be seen in illustration 166, page 115.)

181. Worn runners. Note the troughs in the runners and veneer loss and wear on the front rail.

"Force and Fix" Reparations

There are several methods of dealing with warped core wood, depending on whether a veneered section is to be removed first. Boards may be flattened by mechanical pressure or by changing the humidity, but any attempt to return the board to its original shape by means of steaming or wetting the board will only provide a temporary remedy—the board will return to its warped condition when it dries out.

A more permanent cure can be achieved by pulling the board flat and securing it in place. This "force and fix" technique is most likely to succeed if: (a) the board is not too hard, (b) the board is not too thick, (c) there is something substantial to secure the board to and (d) the

additional supports will not spoil the appearance of the piece. The back of the board is wetted either by steam or by covering with wet sawdust and left overnight. The board is then fastened between four cross-bearers which are progressively tightened. Or, as an alternative, the back is well sized and hand-veneered, with plenty of moisture on the veneer backing, and clamped flat under pressure and allowed to dry out for a long period. When the panel is released from pressure, it is immediately fastened securely to the core.

If the panel is veneered and the original veneer is not to be removed, or the board is too thick to flatten by either of the above methods, the board should be grooved. If the veneer has been removed, the board may be sawed into narrow strips, planed true and edge-jointed so that

182. Repaired runners. The troughs have been filled in and the veneer replaced. The drawer now travels on the runner smoothly.

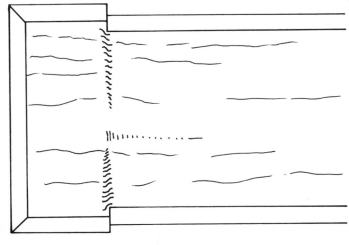

183. Veneer buckling due to core wood reduction or shrinkage.

alternate strips have their heartwood sides opposed to equalize and distribute their different tendencies to curvature—and thus warping. (Remember, sapwood has a higher moisture content than heartwood, so that distribution of moisture in the cut board varies. The moist parts will shrink more than the drier parts causing the possibility of warpage.) It may be necessary to add a further strip to make up the original width. The whole is then planed level, resulting in a slightly thinner board.

When the board is thin, it is often possible to hand-veneer the back in strips, leaving about 4″ between strips 6″ wide. This will enable the amount of pull to be controlled. Further strips can be added as necessary. Sometimes veneer strips laid diagonally to the corners will correct a minor warp.

"Doubling-up" Reparations

When a board is wormy or defective in other ways, such as from insect attack or rot, it is sometimes practical to plane off the old board, down to a thickness of 3/16″, and bond a new board to this remaining original. This bonding should be accomplished by gluing the heart side (the stronger side) of the new board (well seasoned and of proper kind) to the remains of the old one.

This "doubling-up" technique can also be used to cure a warped veneer section. Sometimes a combination of methods gives best results. Where the section can be removed completely, slots are sawn in the back and the whole is flattened. After strips have been glued into the

Repairs and Restoration · 127

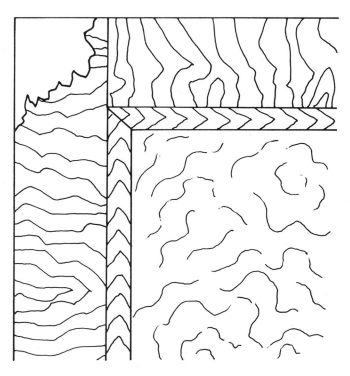

184. Typical veneer damage to a surface corner resulting from abuse or loss of adhesion at the glue line.

slots, a backing board is bonded heart-side to the original.

If a new board has to be used as a completely new replacement, it should be well-seasoned, radially cut timber. If only one veneer is to be used, it is laid on the heartside with the minimum of moisture or heat. Wherever possible, an under-veneer is first laid across the grain, and the face veneer laid with the grain. For best work, both sides of the board should have under-veneers, and the backing veneer should be of the same strength and width as the face veneer and laid at the same time.

Reparation of Edges and Corners

More common faults of veneer occur in corners and edges, as these are easily chipped. Areas which are handled frequently, or where moving parts create friction, such as drawer and door edges, are very prone to damage. Drawer rails often suffer in this way, particularly when the veneer is thin. (An example of such damage can be seen in illustration 139 on page 95.) However, much old furniture veneer was as much as ⅛″ thick and more in the nature of a facing. As seen in Chapter 10, in all early work the veneer was sawn by hand, and during the 19th and early 20th centuries the best veneers were saw-cut by machine rather than sliced by knife. Today, it is difficult to buy saw-cut veneer and it is often necessary to saw veneers by hand or on a circular saw to enable a repair to be completed.

The treatment for a chipped corner or edge depends largely upon the grain and figure of the veneer. If it is of a curly, well-marked variety, the cabinetmaker endeavors to follow it as far as possible, selecting a new patch which matches as closely as it can.

To make a pattern for the new veneer, a piece of paper is held over the corner and the heel ball is rubbed over it, thus making the outline. The new veneer is held in a position to give the nearest match of grain, and the paper stuck to it. The outline is cut round with a fine fret-saw and finally trimmed to shape by trial and error with a file. When ready, it is glued into position and rubbed down, with tape stuck over the joint to prevent it from opening as the glue dries out. If it does tend to lift, a flat block can be warmed and clamped over it with news-paper between. (This softens the glue again so that it will hold.) It is desirable for new veneer to be slightly thicker than the old so that it can be levelled later without interference to the surrounding surface.

Veneered drawer rails frequently suffer damage, either due to the drawer itself catching the veneer or because of excessive wear at the ends. (See illustration 181.) This veneer should be relatively thick but, regardless of its thickness, it is essential that the worn wood at the back be made good and sound first. Usually straight-grain veneer is used on these rails.

Blisters and Bruises

When veneer has lifted locally in the form of a blister, it usually implies that the glue beneath has perished. Thus it is of little use to apply a hot caul over it. What is necessary is the introduction of fresh glue. In order to accomplish this, the cabinetmaker makes a cut through the blister following the grain direction. This cut enables the veneer at each side to be pressed down so that glue can be introduced by a slip of veneer or a thin palette knife. After gluing, it is important to clamp a warm block over the surface with newspaper interposed. It can usually be established whether or not the veneer is down properly by tapping with the fingernails—a hollow sound will be heard when the veneer is still raised.

Bruises in a veneered surface can be difficult to cope with in that any attempt to raise the bruise by steaming may result in the veneer being lifted. Unless the bruising is really bad, it may be best to leave it as it is. Otherwise, it is necessary to prick the surface right through the polish and veneer, place a damp rag over the affected area and apply a hot iron so that steam reaches the groundwork,

185. Poorly matched veneer repair—in grain direction, wood type, figure and color—for the top surface of this chest of drawers. Note the unfortunately irregular shapes of the repair pieces.

tending to swell it. Unfortunately, apart from the danger of the veneer lifting, the surface finish may deteriorate, requiring further treatment.

THE REPARATION OF MARQUETRY

The repair of marquetry can be troublesome, particularly when entire pieces are missing. Usually, replacements must be made by the repairer himself, involving much work and challenge. Elaborate designs may be beyond the capacity of the cabinetmaker, but simple fan corner pieces, for example, can be recreated. The tapered pieces are prepared first and fitted together. They are usually shaded toward one edge, and this is done by holding each individual piece with a tweezer and dipping it into hot sand (similar to the heated sand used by the optician in adjusting eyeglasses).

Sometimes marquetry panels have lifted in parts—often resulting in the disappearance of small pieces. If the missing pieces are not too large, replacements can be

fitted into position, working from a traced outline of the design. In cases where the marquetry has lifted badly, however, the treatment may be difficult. The repairer can attempt to clamp a hot caul over the raised part, but usually the glue beneath has perished and fresh glue has to be worked in if possible. This is usually feasible when the bubble is at the edge, or when one of the pieces of marquetry has come adrift, the glue being worked in with a scrap of veneer.

When the bubble/blister is a small local one, it is often possible to remove a piece of veneer either entirely or sufficiently for fresh glue to be inserted. When a large area has come adrift, the only satisfactory action is to raise the whole, clean off the old glue, and lay it afresh. In raising veneer for regluing, a spatula or similar flat knife should always be the first method the cabinetmaker tries for loosening the glue. Applied heat for this purpose may destroy the surface patina and finish.

One of the difficulties in working with lifted pieces of veneer and their replacements is the possibility of the replaced veneer getting out of position. Really large areas of lifted parquetry or marquetry are extremely difficult to deal with and may necessitate a hot caul being pressed

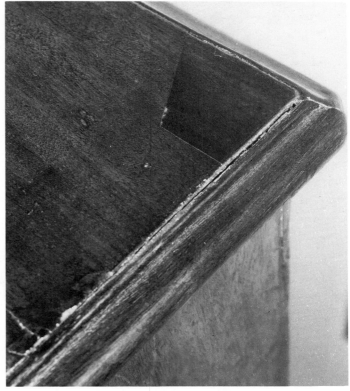

186. Well-matched veneer patch repair: the grain direction is the same, the kind and figure of the wood is similar, and the color is quite close. The lines of the repair are as unnoticeable as possible.

Repairs and Restoration · 129

187. *Lifted veneer.*

188. *Veneer blister probably due to perished glue.*

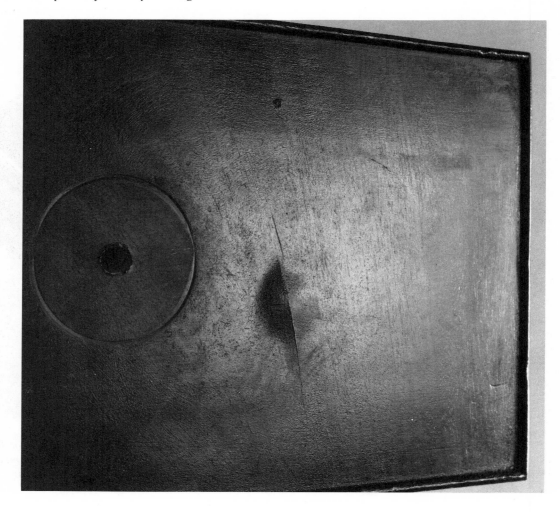

over the entire surface to soften the glue. In order to preserve the pattern and parts, gummed tape should first be laid over the inlay or a thin piece of brown paper should be glued over it to hold the parts together. This is a very difficult operation and should be avoided if possible.

Brass inlay, especially stringing, sometimes causes complications when solid groundwork shrinks across the grain. The brass is unable to accommodate itself to the reduced size and lifts, forming small loops (see illustration 189). It is impossible to press down on the loop as the groove is too short or narrow for the brass. The only solution is to cut across the inlay with a line hacksaw (or metal-cutting saw). The saw cut generally removes enough metal to enable the parts to be pressed down but, if necessary, the cut ends can be filed down a bit. The brass tends to be springy so that the repairer usually clamps a block over the inlay while the glue sets. Similar problems occur with wood string inlay owing to the core wood shrinkage, and similar action must be taken for correction of the difficulty.

COMBATING DAMPNESS

Occasionally a piece of furniture has been stored in a damp cellar or barn and requires attention. Typical damp-induced problems include drawers and doors which stick or bind, stiff table leaves, rusted hardware, buckled veneer, failure of glued parts in general, and a deteriorated finish.

The absorption of damp is a fairly slow process, made still slower by the finish on the piece, which acts as a barrier. Movement in the wood is therefore very slow and any attempt at putting things right should be slow as well. If movement is speeded up, as it would be if the wood were brought into a hot room and left there, the glue would probably fail immediately, with resulting loose joints. One should not attempt to reglue failed joints while they are still damp, as the glue will not hold properly.

Furniture is rarely affected by dry rot unless it has been

189. Early 19th-century card table with decorative brass inlay stringing. Note corner where brass has lifted and looped.

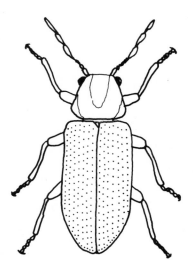

190. Woodworm: *the larva (or grub) stage of the furniture beetle ("worm") and the adult beetle. The most common furniture beetle or woodworm,* Anobium punctatum, *is dark reddish brown in color and measures ½" in length with parallel rows of small pits in the wing cases. The earlier stage of grub or worm is cream color.*

stored in a damp, unventilated cellar. Once badly attacked, a piece cannot be repaired because the substance of the wood itself has deteriorated. Molds and mildew can grow on the surface of wood and may stain it, but usually will not cause serious damage.

WORMHOLES

When small holes appear on the surface of old furniture, chances are that the woodworm has been at work. "Woodworm" is the term commonly applied to the species of grub or larva which germinates in wood and tunnels through, devouring and turning it to powder. Wood-boring insects generally called woodworms include the beetle families of Anobiidae, Lyctidae and Bostrichidae. Once the presence of woodworm has been detected, treatment should begin at once. Even if the surface of affected wood shows nothing more than a few tiny holes (about 1/16" in diameter), the interior of the piece may be half eaten away. Hardwoods and softwoods, including pines, are liable to attack under proper conditions; walnut and beech in particular suffer, whereas mahogany and oak seem almost immune.

The beetles may have been introduced from other furniture or they may have entered through an open window, since they live in the dead branches of trees. The female lays her eggs in crevices in the wood, then dies. Small grubs hatch from the eggs and begin to burrow into the wood. They work along in this way for perhaps a year or two, leaving behind them a channel filled with a light, fine powder. Finally, the grub tunnels toward the surface of the wood and bores a chamber in which it lies until it turns into a chrysalis. After a few weeks it develops into a

mature beetle with wings and legs, bites its way through to the wood's surface and emerges. Thus, what we call a wormhole is actually a flight hole. This exodus generally takes place during June, July and August, although it may occur as early as May. The male and female beetles mate and the entire process starts again.

The presence of holes is not proof that beetles are still at work, but it is usually possible to detect recent holes by their appearance—i.e., the edges will be sharp and the insides light yellow. Holes caused by an old colony which had died out are usually dark and half-filled with furniture wax.

The most common treatment for woodworm is the application of oil-borne organochlorine insecticides made especially for this purpose. Before application, as much powder as possible should be removed from the holes to enable the liquid to penetrate. The liquid is fed into the holes with a small brush or funnel. One treatment may not suffice since individual beetles may escape.

Another method of treatment (which does involve sending the infected furniture to a firm with the necessary equipment) is that of fumigation. The furniture is placed in a special chamber, which is then filled with a poisonous gas. This elaborate measure does not, however, prevent future attack. Action should be taken at the first signs of infection.

Where wormholes exist, the most important thing to establish is how far the structural strength of the afflicted piece has deteriorated. When the attack is only slight it is enough to treat the wood with an insecticide. If structural parts have been badly damaged, the only alternative is to replace them with sound wood, taking the precaution of rubbing the new wood with insecticide. Such affected parts as rails can sometimes be backed with sound wood, this backing being joined or screwed to whatever adjoining members there may be and glued on. This is often the procedure for veneered parts, for example, which may be unmarked on the surface but badly worm-eaten in the core wood beneath.

When a part such as a leg is so badly attacked as to be liable to snap off, and the item is required for a further period of service, there is little to be done except to replace the affected part. Sometimes it is possible to make a reasonably effective repair by cutting a groove at the back of a leg and letting in a sound strip of wood. This would enable a piece such as a side cabinet or light bureau to stand and be used, but would be of little value for a chair or table in constant service.

Repairs such as the above are relatively simple matters of replacement and fitting. It is when the "show wood" or primary wood surface is affected by woodworm that the problem becomes really serious.

PROTECTION AND CARE

Prudent care and protection should be assumed for all antique furniture. Carelessness and risk of danger should never be permitted with fine old pieces which are irreplaceable, regardless of money, skill or time. Among the simple precautions to be taken are the following. Old furniture should be kept away from strong sunlight and never left on a porch or patio. One should never stand on an old chair, especially if it has a cane or rush seat. Feet should be kept off chair rungs and trestle-table bases. Desk tops made of soft pine should be covered with a blotter to avoid pen and pencil dents. And, when a loose joint is discovered or a section of veneer comes open, it should receive the immediate attention of a cabinetmaker to avoid progressive problems.

Despite normal household cleanliness, dust, dirt and grime find their way onto all flat surfaces. This, coupled with dampness, fireplace smoke, cooking vapors and cigar smoke, produces a thin film on furniture. To maintain maximum beauty, this film must be removed. A light dusting with a clean, soft cloth once or twice a week should accomplish this. About once every six months, a mild furniture wax or cream polish might be applied to surfaces in very small quantities. However, the less one puts on one's furniture, thereby minimizing buildup, the better.

Although the debate continues in the art-historical community as to whether to polish the furniture brasses or not, if the decision is to polish, remove the tarnished brasses from the furniture before the procedure. (Be sure to note the location of every pull, screw and nut, each unique, so as to return them to their original places.)

191. *Replacement pad foot on worm-ridden table leg.*

Cleaning/polishing hardware on the piece abrades the surrounding finish and allows polishing agents to run beneath the hardware where they can damage the metal and the finish. Coating the newly polished brasses with a lacquer-type product will prolong the time between polishings.

As mentioned earlier, in the United States and elsewhere, where low winter temperatures demand intense central heating, a problem is created due to changes in temperature and humidity. The drying central heat reduces the humidity content which, in turn, causes the furniture to dry out, crack and shrink. Mechanical humidifiers seem one of the best counterbalancing devices for replacing the moisture content, although some wood movement is inevitable. Ideal is a constant relative humidity of 50 percent and a constant temperature of about 45 degrees F.

Dramatic wood movement often takes place when a piece of furniture of 200–300 years in age is permanently moved from one climate to another—from damp England to relatively dry Boston, for example. Little can be done to avoid or protect against such movement, and it is difficult to guess how severely a piece will be affected. In fact, it is a game of chance. When the adjustments have taken place (and this takes a year or more), a respected cabinetmaker should be consulted concerning any necessary restoration or repair.

Chapter 14

Upholstery

UPHOLSTERY COVERING FOR SEAT furniture has traditionally been of interest to collectors, museum curators and furniture scholars, in terms of expressing their personal tastes and to add attractiveness to particular room settings. In some situations historic textiles, such as curtains, dresses or tapestry fragments, have been used for covering to add mellow historic effect and to complement with something of age and beauty, often documented somewhat to period use in paintings and prints (see illustration 95, page 65). Historic trade sources, such as textile design books and bills or ledgers, can tell us what was available for use, but almost never are there original show cover textiles surviving on historic furniture. Textiles have limited lives, no matter how little they are used, since they deteriorate naturally, and since reupholstery was an easy way to keep in fashion.

Until the past few years, emphasis has been primarily on the look of the covering: its weave type, its design, and its color. Commercial fabric manufacturers have encouraged this by reproducing historic documents, sometimes as authentic weave and structural weight in accurate color, scale and complete design, but often in barely recognizable adaptations confusing to the potential user. Fortunately for today's furniture scholars, many manufacturers are providing more information about a textile's original use and its historic document color, as well as the production changes in design and scale which may have been necessary for machine capability or sometimes because of the economics of marketplace demand.

Study of historic upholstery during the past ten years has extended beyond interest in correct color, design and weave to deal with the treatment of the upholstery, i.e., not only what was utilized but also how it was utilized, and therefore what it more likely looked like per designer's or maker's original intentions. This new dimension of furniture study includes the understanding and study of upholstery techniques, both modern and historic approaches, as well as the vast variety of upholstery treatment design options. Once again, historic reference materials are examined and analyzed for further information. Such awareness results in greater interest and sensitivity about the upholstery one encounters on historic furniture.

The challenging search for accurate documentation and the pleasure of appropriate upholstery decisions for his own historic pieces of furniture is a collector's responsibility and reward. Outer show cover choice as

192. *Empire sofa, Boston, Massachusetts, mahogany, circa 1825–1835, reupholstery treatment using green satin reproduction textile, based on an historic print of the period which documents a contemporary fashionable upholstery treatment for a very similar sofa design. Gift of Colonel and Mrs. Thomas R. West. Photograph courtesy the Museum of Fine Arts, Boston.*

193. *Plate 9 in the popular London periodical, Rudolph Ackermann's* The Repository of Arts, Literature, Commerce, Manufactures, Fashions, and Politics, *vol. 2, no. 61 (January 1821). Hand-colored apple-green aquatint and engraving of "Dress Sofa," designed by J. Taylor, meaning a formal, elegant piece suitable for the parlor. Photograph by Daniel Farber.*

well as the undercover stuffing materials and treatment affect the molded shape and the proportions of a Chippendale sofa, for example, and the trained eye of today's furniture scholar recognizes this importance. Earlier in this century the general approach was for overall overstuffed upholstery treatments, thereby losing frame outline and proportions to a chubby look. Many historic period treatments were selectively lean, emphasizing line contours and maintaining good proportions, perhaps at the price of slightly less comfort by today's standards. In contrast, a frequent error in the reupholstery of 18th-century French seating furniture is the lack of sufficient foundation and cushioning thickness to thus provide the original historic appearance.

194. Philadelphia easy chair, circa 1765–1790, with surviving partial original underupholstery and selective padding to maintain frame outline and proportions, i.e., the back bows out slightly and the wings bulge inward, yet the edges of the wings and the crest rail are bare except for the canvas cover. The left-side later damask show cover documents an early 20th-century Colonial-revival covering. Courtesy Collection of Peter W. Eliot.

195. Fauteuil open armchair, French, carved and gilded walnut frame, signed by Georges Jacob, circa 1780. White satin upholstery cover, circa 1830 or later, embroidered with colored silks, the floral design in the style of Philippe de la Salle (1723–1805), prominent Lyons silk designer and manufacturer. The Metropolitan Museum of Art, Gift of the Samuel H. Kress Foundation, 1958.

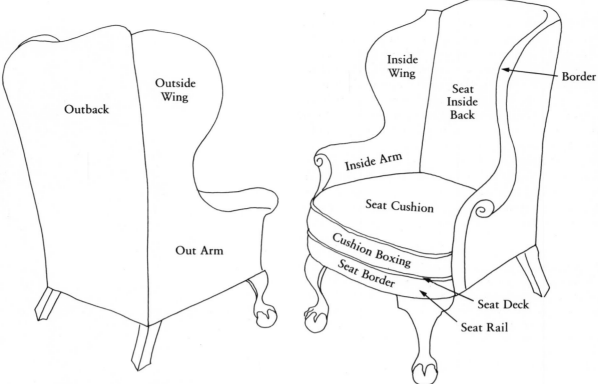

196. *Upholstery terms for the components of a chair. Drawing by Ellen Rosenthal.*

ELEMENTS OF ASSEMBLY

Historically the upholsterer was the master craftsman responsible for the upholstery decisions, as well as their implementation. He was of strong persuasion and his work was held in high regard, because until 19th-century industrialized production of textiles, the upholstery was several times more costly than the chair frame, even when the frame was carved or embellished. Careful plans and all upholsterer mistakes were critical.

Upholstery terms for individual components of a frame clarify location and function. The "outback," for example, refers to the upholstery textile on the outside back of a piece, likewise the "out arms," the "seat back" is that portion of an upholstered piece where one's back rests, and the "seat deck" is the seat upholstery under a loose cushion. "Tight seats" can be either slip seats, which have a loose upholstered frame held by inner seat rail rabbets, or fixed upholstery carried over the seat rails (see illustration 134, page 90). The overall outer fabric covering is known as the "show cover," "finish fabric" or "upholstery covering," and beneath is the "under-upholstery" or "undercover," which consists of stitching, cover, stuffing, springs, sackcloth and webbing. The "cake" is the 20th-century term used to define this stitched-together combination of unseen foundation materials. The shaping of its edges and crown can also provide clues to upholstery treatment. It is part of the history of the chair, and should therefore be preserved, although it is an aspect which has not been considered until recent times, especially by the upholstery trade.

High-backed cane and bannister-back early baroque ("Pilgrim")-style New England chairs, introduced in the 1690s, usually had grass stuffing supported by linen webbing and sackcloth and held in place by double stitching; contemporary European upholsterers were also using curled horsehair, tow (broken flax stems), etc. Imported from northern Russia via London, refined Russian leather, with its faint incised-diamond surface pattern, was a desirable and durable show covering of this period, as was English woven polychrome floral turkey-work, knotted and evenly clipped to create pile like a carpet. Cushions were made with a ticking case stuffed with a down and quill mixture called "feathers." Surviving examples of loom-woven show cover textiles often have wonderful companion fringes, and when upturned, they sometimes reveal underupholstery with widely spaced narrow strips of linen webbing interlaced to form an open lattice in the English manner, or broad strips closely interwoven in the French manner.

197. Slip seat, Boston, 1755–1775: (a) with original girt webbing and linen sackcloth bottom nailed to slip-seat framework; (b) same slip seat showing the historic stuffing of grass and curled horsehair and outer layer of linen.

198. Turkey-work upholstery cover original to Boston couch, circa 1697–1698, with polychrome flowers on black background (now perished) and some surviving fragments of fringe along the seat rail. Courtesy The Essex Institute.

a.

b.

199. *Two types of seat webbing: (a) English manner of widely spaced interlaced webbing strips; (b) French manner of closely interwoven strips of linen webbing. Drawings by Ellen Rosenthal.*

200. *Seat rail with brass close nailing pattern of decorative swags and drops, characteristic of Federal-period chairs. Side chair, Salem, circa 1790, attributed to William Fiske (1770–1844). Courtesy The Society for the Preservation of New England Antiquities.*

Decorative brass nails frequently enhanced the show covers—never "brass tacks" because, in fact, there is no such thing as a brass tack, hence the incorrectness of the expression "sharp as a brass tack"; tacks were made of iron, were used to hold underupholstery layers to the frame, and were not meant to be seen. The Anglo-American upholstery tradition (as opposed to the Iberian and Dutch practices, where leather seats and backs were secured by large brass nails called "bullions") reserved brass nails for ornamental effects, using plain cast brass heads of low profile with tapered brass shanks. The head undersides were left rough, to cut costs and to provide a better grip on the upholstery covering. On stripped frames, it is often possible to identify the original nailing pattern from the remaining shanks of broken-off nails, remaining tack holes from prior upholsteries, whose shape is also a dating clue, and faint impressions of the former nail heads.

The upholstery trade in the 18th century was lucrative and the most prestigious of the furniture-making crafts. This was a factor of the continuing reality of great textile cost, which was at least three times that of the frame. Citations in historic probate documents record the upholstered easy chair and fully hung bedstead as being most highly valued. It is known that Louis XIV discarded gilded chair frames when the silk upholstery show covers were worn.

201. Nailing patterns can often be identified from the shapes of surviving nail shank holes: (left) 18th-century irregular wrought-iron nail hole, (center) 19th-century cut-nail hole and (right) circular shank hole of machined late 19th-century wire nail.

202. Original floral needlework on compass slip seat, Boston Queen Anne chair, circa 1730–1740, wool on linen. Life-size scale and strong jewel-tone colors were characteristic of the mid-18th century. Photograph courtesy the Museum of Fine Arts, Boston.

203. "Watered" worsted wool moreen original slip seat show cover, mahogany side chair, Portsmouth, New Hampshire, or York, Maine, 1760–1775. Courtesy The Society for the Preservation of New England Antiquities.

The so-called "upholders" served as the general decorators of the 18th century, being both merchants and craftsmen who supplied complete and appropriate furnishings to a household, thus becoming arbiters of taste. Usually from prominent families, upholders pursued their many options with good taste and confidence; prototype documents and survivals of their work are considered desirable guidelines even today. Stylish upholstery show cover fabrics might occasionally include expensive silk damask or needlework, though mostly stiff worsted wool known as "herateen," "cheney" or "moreen" (sometimes "watered," a surface finishing technique intended to impart the look of more costly silk moire), as well as prints, checks and woven blackish horsehair (never totally black because horsehair cannot take dye evenly).

Copperplate printing, introduced in England during the 1750s, prompted greater interest in and availability of printed cottons and linens by 1800. The plates recorded popular newsworthy subjects such as the first balloon ascent in 1783. Trimmings included decorative tapes (historically called "binding"), used on American easy chairs, for example, as well as the many French upholstery trimmings called "passementerie," which included cords, fringes and tassels designed to enhance the glorious silk upholstery covers. Curled horsehair became the usual foundation stuffing (and continues to be today, preferred though expensive) because it retained its loft and better stayed in place.

Eighteenth-century upholstery treatments were carefully planned, effective and interesting, and many are still used today, alas frequently not so effectively. Prudent use of costly upholstery show cover or finish fabric can be recognized, for example, on Provincial French chair frames upholstered in silk. These chairs often have the less visible open outback covered with less expensive check linen.

The development of the underupholstery edge roll technique allowed 18th-century upholsterers to achieve a more controlled contour treatment. Linen sleeves were

204. Silk upholstered French chair frame; the open outback often had a show cover of less expensive checked linen.

205. The easy chair wing underupholstery edge roll technique allowed the upholsterer to refine and control the upholstery contours.

206. *Stitched edge foundation underupholstery, a so-called "French edge," provided the stiff boxed upholstery outlines fashionable in the late 18th-century neoclassic taste.*

207. *Tufted and buttoned upholstery treatment, the tufting pattern carefully planned to complement the shape of the Renaissance-revival-style circa 1860s side-chair back. Original velvet show cover and underupholstery; sometimes contrasting color covered buttons were used for stylish effect.*

stuffed with grass and then tacked to the edges of easy chair wings, arms and front seat rails. This treatment created smooth, exact lines, protected the show cover from needless wear produced by a sharp frame edge, and also protected the sitter from the hard wooden frame.

The late 18th-century neoclassic taste for rectilinear forms prompted the development of upholstery foundations with stiff boxed outlines, best known as a "French edge," though the French historically called this treatment "la piqûre à l'Anglaise," so who knows where the square stitched edge technique first began? To prevent these squared edges from being crushed out of shape through use, elaborate stitching plans were evolved to reinforce the square walls of the foundations. Four types of stitching were used: surface quilting, in which the mass of horsehair stuffing in the seat was quilted together with through stitches, a second type whereby rows of stitches were passed diagonally through the corners to draw them up into stiff peaks, a third, blind stitching, in which horsehair stuffing was captured with the curved needle

and drawn up against the side walls of the seat, and, finally, a fourth type involving rows of diagonal through stitches which passed through the sides and top of the seat, compressing the horsehair and drawing it up into a stiff, sharp edge. The French working in the late 18th-century Louis XVI style were superb in their execution of stitching plans, and it is not surprising that French upholsterers in New York and Philadelphia first stitched French edges in America in the 1790s.

Decorative mathematically plotted shallow looped tufting patterns began in the mid-18th century, whereby stitching through layers of upholstery stuffing was also a functional method of keeping the underupholstery in place. Elongated stitched channel tufting was a late 18th-century treatment for the seat back of the barrel-back easy chair. (The stripped frame in illustration 94, page 64, would have had such a treatment; note how minimal the frame is on which to upholster.) Deep pleated diamond tufting, a pleated sewn-in method of anchoring stuffing and of elaborating chair surfaces, was likely invented in Paris in the late 1830s or early 1840s. Contrary to its appearance, most pleated tufting was not soft for sitting.

Nineteenth-century pleated tufting and button treatments were an exuberant form of upholstery, requiring considerably more fabric to execute than most treatments. This extravagance reflected the new prosperity which enabled homeowners to afford larger quantities of less costly textiles. There were many remarkable and ingenious variations, including biscuit and bun tufting, which formed rectangles and squares, star tufting, which consisted of diamond shapes that formed a wheel with a single center button, and stitched bustle tufting, a swell at the lower inside back. A large number of examples survive, often in poor condition, to serve as documents for study today. Trade catalogs, periodicals, etc., published in the 19th century, even family photographs such as the Castle Tucker parlor view (illustration 209), provide excellent pictorial information. Further interesting and useful reference sources are the past sale records and sample archives of those manufacturers which continue to produce fabrics today.

Though copper springs were used with limited success as early as the 1830s, and exercise horses of the 18th century utilized springs for mechanical action, spring seats only became basic to all upholstered seating furniture during the last half of the 19th century. About 1850, springs became attractively affordable with improvements in the iron and steel industry, resulting in an increasingly reliable product which offered both comfort and firm shape, and thus a less expensive substitute for the use of great quantities of costly horsehair and time-consuming stitching of edges. In fact, springs were first widely used for public seats in steamboats, trains and hotels where cost and durability were very important.

The use of springs quickly expanded beyond serving as filler for cheap furniture, as upholsterers learned how to use them. They recognized the importance of tying down the spring tops so they moved together as a single seat platform, and welcomed the evolution of the stronger biconical steel spring of hourglass shape, which made for a stiffer spring with more consistent resilience than the earlier conical spring. Hence seats could be deeper and

208. *Iron/wire frame Turkish armchair, circa 1863, seat rails and legs the only wood, being overstuffed with wool rep, diamond and half-diamond tufted and button back and seat and "ruffled" seat and back border upholstery treatments. Elaborate "Turkish" upholstery reached the height of popularity after 1880. Not only did the Turkish chair represent the height of technique and ingenuity among upholsterers, but the "wire frame" turned the entire chair into one desirable resilient spring. The greater amount of workmanship involved to construct a stable seat, given so little frame, made wire frame upholstery more expensive than traditional wood frame upholstery. Courtesy The Society for the Preservation of New England Antiquities. Photograph by J. David Bohl.*

209. This photograph, 1858, of the family parlor, Castle Tucker, Wiscasset, Maine, documents a parlor suite of commercial furniture acquired in Boston in 1858 which survives in situ. A side chair from the suite stands in front of the photograph. The original button-tufted satin-weave wool (satin-de-laine) upholstery show fabric was printed to look like more costly brocaded silk damask. Courtesy Castle Tucker House Museum.

210. *Spring tops tied down together so that they move together as a unified seat and provide consistent resilience. Drawing by Ellen Rosenthal.*

211. *Custom Spanish chair with handsomely carved frame and fancy upholstery fabrics and treatment, button-tufted brown mohair plush and inserted polychrome needlework panel, circa 1860–1880. Courtesy The Society for the Preservation of New England Antiquities. Photograph by J. David Bohl.*

more comfortable than in earlier upholstery techniques.

Rapidly, upholsterers developed improved and varied techniques for spring tying, such as double-strand twine and "return" tying, more effective knots and the use of lashing, which is the running of twine diagonally across the springs to provide additional stability to springs already tied front to back and side to side. Firmly securing springs in these ways assured their moving together as a unified seat, and therefore reduced problems caused by springs rubbing against one another or by the twine chafing and wearing away.

The spring foundation improvements were catapulted into use by the increased demand for upholstered furniture in the mid-19th century. A prosperous and growing middle class was eager for consumer goods; actively producing textile mills and furniture factories were eager to supply.

In great contrast to the contemporary inexpensive mass-production factory upholstery operations, there were expensive custom shops, working in traditional methods and using costly materials, who simply adapted springs into their furniture, i.e., springs would be stitched to linen webbing and covered with a layer of sackcloth upon which was made a hair-stuffed cake with stitched edges. This technique produced resilient seats and dramatic contours for elaborate show cover fabrics. The craftsman skill and time necessary to correctly tie the springs, to compact the hair evenly using the regulator needle, to stitch the edge tightly and to lay out and stuff the show cover properly far exceeded earlier demands on the upholsterer. Many of these pieces of furniture featured quilting, tufting, channeling and pleating treatments involving yet more skill and time. It is not surprising to note that the 19th century is often deemed "The Age of Upholstery."

Also at this time, commercial upholstery shops were engaged in cost-conscious middle-range operations which compromised on materials and techniques: stronger but short-lived jute and burlap for linen webbing and covers, minimal tying of springs, simulated stitched square edge using reed edges or steel wire, and imitation textile show cover fabrics (see the Castle Tucker parlor furniture, illustration 209). Plain black horsehair was one of the two most popular middle-class show cover upholstery fabrics between 1850 and 1875. It was sturdy and resisted insect damage, yet it offered a satisfying high sheen like the silk on very expensive furniture. (The other was heavily woven rep in plain colors, illustration 208, often with colored stripes.) Counterpart shops today indiscriminately use staple guns and foam rubber!

Mechanical upholstery devices developed in the late 19th/early 20th century with the emphasis on cutting labor time and therefore cost. There were power-press tufting machines, for example, which produced a continuous pad of show cover, stuffing and undercover, and

212. Gimp trimmings, 19th century. The upper trimming, wool wrapped over vellum, is called "embassy" gimp. Beneath, "shell" gimp trim, which serves as a heading for the fringe, is asymmetrical to thus be possible to be applied to curved edges. Note the fringe hand-tied knot each strand, designed to make small tassels. Courtesy The Society for the Preservation of New England Antiquities. Photograph by J. David Bohl.

213. *Commercial shop parlor suite, photograph in advertising mailer from "M. & H. Schrenkeisen/Furniture Manufacturers / 23 to 29 Elizabeth St. / New York," circa* 1880–1885. *Pleated tufting and crowned spring seat upholstery treatments were standard for such "Aesthetic" furniture of the time. Courtesy Smithsonian Institution.*

WAL'ONLY   N°222   FULL-SIZE

were simply applied and nailed over the edges of the furniture frame without relating to the lines of the piece. Commercial shops and low-end factory operations increasingly utilized prefabricated mass-produced steel components, replacing all attempts at twine-tied springs with steel conical springs, webbing with steel bands, and steel-wire edges for stitched definitions. These steel components were connected by steel clamps and the assembled units were thinly covered with burlap, cotton batting skimmer fill, and show cover fabric, all ready for placing in any frame of counterpart size. Early in the 20th century these "factory units" were widely used and applauded. Their success was in part due to the developing automobile industry, which created and increased demand for cushion seats.

UPHOLSTERY CONCERNS

The conservation and preservation of upholstery on historic furniture and on contemporary pieces prevail today for many of the same reasons: concern for comfort, aesthetic design appreciation, and awareness of high upholstery costs. The search for all available historic upholstery evidence, such as fabric fiber content and its specific color, layer, etc., must be recognized, and, whatever the reupholstery compromises, this evidence should be preserved for future documentation, interpretation and reupholstery consideration.

Seating frame rails are weakened with additional splintered wood and loss areas by each upholstery

214. Adjustable "Roman Divan" couch with high back, cheaply upholstered mass-produced factory piece, circa 1900–1915. The printed voided cotton velveteen original cover with stamped metal trim in imitation of brass nailing has been tufted by machine and then applied to the frame, apparent by the regularity of the buttons without regard to spacing placement. Underside machine evidence shows a regular pattern of buttons clenched with metal shanks through round washers. The back was done by a more skilled factory worker, section work having been introduced in the 1890s. Courtesy of The Margaret Woodbury Strong Museum.

215. *Piano stool, walnut, Renaissance-revival style, circa 1860–1870, with original crushed mohair plush and "bouillon" fringe upholstery show cover. Courtesy, Gibson House Museum, Boston.*

216. *Side chair, Philadelphia, commissioned by John Cadwalader, attributed to Thomas Affleck, circa 1770. Removable self-contained upholstery seat cap which fits onto the seat frame without further intrusive self-destructive tacks and nails. Courtesy, The Henry Francis duPont Winterthur Museum.*

generation of tacking and brass nailing, in fact a self-destructive process. The importance of preserving the frame is major. Traditionally, linen saturated with glue has been placed over prior tack holes for consolidating strength and stability, as shown in illustration 94, page 64. Today Japanese paper is frequently used in the same manner for the same purpose. Modern use of snap and Velcro closures has reduced areas of tacking and its damage to frames, an especially desirable technique for museum presentations, where use need not be considered. In fact, professional museum upholstery conservators have recently devised ingenious totally noninvasive treatments, using modern semirigid Ethafoam, as self-contained shaped upholstery units called caps, which fit onto a framework or drop into a seat without tacks or nails anew. Certainly putting decorative nails and tacks into existing holes assures no new holes to further weaken the frame rails. It is possible to slipcover a chair or sofa and have it look reupholstered, a practical tradition dating back to the 18th century which can serve as a nonintervention treatment today. When an important seat form with its original upholstery is recognized as having historic significance and its condition is fragile, retirement from active use may be the best preservation plan. Giving the chair with its upholstery (or just the upholstery alone) to an interested museum would extend its limited longevity.

Upholstery wear, use and the environment determine its life. Some conservation problems, such as bugs (clothes moths and carpet beetles, for examples), can be eliminated and guarded against. Air pollution problems of the modern age also affect textiles, so that dusting and light vacuuming are helpful maintenance. Pet stains and liquid stains should be removed so as to avoid a "tide line," i.e., the stain edge (line) is stiff and will cause a break in the textile over time, therefore this demarcation line should at least be softened with cleaning. Photo-chemical damage (sunlight in particular), whether to a strong new textile or a weak historic one, is devastating, and results in fading, deterioration, and even disappearance! Bad frame repairs can also affect both the show cover and the underupholstery; staples, replacement wood, additive nonoriginal springs and make-do home solutions may quickly prove counterproductive. Cambric, thin black cloth nailed to seat rail bottom edges, is theoretically used to catch dust as springs act, but it also serves as a cover-up device for the upholsterer and should in fact be removed for better watchfulness to changes in the upholstery.

Chapter 15

Fakes

A SPURIOUS PIECE OF furniture is an imitation of an old piece presented with the intention of deceiving. (The straightforward copying of old examples for sale as reproductions is legitimate commercial business and quite a different matter.) Regardless of how successful the deception may be, the collector must realize that what he is paying so dearly for is the product of modern labor and materials. The piece in question is likely to be inaccurate in historical detail and certainly does not reflect the inherent beauty and character of the past.

Many clever efforts have been made with regard to "faking" antiques. Various techniques have been employed and special pieces which were desirable at certain periods in history have been especially vulnerable to copying. Naturally, such attempts have met with varying degrees of success. The matter of faking furniture is a fascinating subject in its own right and its study provides many valuable cautionary lessons.

217. Early 18th-century joint stool of Massachusetts maple. The use and wear of time can be seen on the worn stretchers, the warped top, and the smoothed thumb-nail molding of the top.

152

218. Twentieth-century oak joint stool with no signs of wear or warpage: the stretchers have received little abuse, the top is straight, and the top edge thumb-nail molding is crisp. The roundels on the apron rails have been carved freely with much contrived irregularity, when in fact a 17th-century counterpart would be symmetrically exact, the carver having laid out the pattern with a compass.

KINDS OF FAKE FURNITURE

A fraudulent old piece may take several forms. This piece may be of entirely new construction—an imitation made from old wood or from wood given the signs of age artificially. Another category of fake is an imitation made up partially of genuine old furniture parts with additions or restorations carried out in new or old material. New carving and other embellishments may be executed on plain but authentic old pieces so as to enhance their value. Another form that is most successful in its deception is the piece created by the transformation of genuine old pieces or parts of them into objects of much greater value by their union with other genuine old pieces or parts of them. The result is sometimes called a "married" piece. The parts of two pieces not made together, however, will seldom "marry" without some alteration to one or both, and it is for the signs of such alterations or inconsistencies that the collector must look. For example, are the primary and secondary woods the same throughout the piece and are the construction details of all drawers (dovetails, back joints, etc.) identical? Are the decorative details (such as crispness of carving) consistent throughout the piece? Do all the brass holes measure alike and do the brasses themselves show signs of similar age? As one approaches the Dunlap highboy pictured here (illustration 220), at first glance one might conclude that all was in order in terms of Dunlap style characteristics and general proportions. But closer study will reveal many inconsistencies that finally lead to the conclusion that this is a married piece. The selected detail of proof, shown in illustration 221, is a comparison of the drawer dovetail joinery for the top and

bottom parts. Obvious differences in size and craftsmanship, top and bottom, indicate that they were certainly not all made by the same furniture craftsman. (Note the variations in drawer size.)

Similar close examination should be applied to matched sets of chairs, particularly if the set is large and complete and thus very rare. Small sets of four are sometimes enlarged to eight by combining old parts with new. This can be highly deceptive when done well, and even though new parts are detected, they can be mistaken for repairs. Each chair must thus be studied carefully.

Whatever the form in which the falsified piece is found, it will be likely to approximate a rare and costly piece in great demand, for only such pieces justify by their financial return the time and effort spent by the faker—a useful thing to remember. Another general point that collectors should keep in mind is that rooms were larger in the past and thus pieces of small size and scale were rare and should be regarded with suspicion. Conversely, the likelihood of buying a large piece of furniture which is later proven spurious is relatively remote. Sideboards, for example, which seem very large by today's standards, are likely to be their original size; a small sideboard in contrast, should be inspected for signs of being cut down.

THE FAKING OF DETAIL WORK

The more wonderful and rare the piece, the more it requires careful scrutiny by the collector to establish its validity. He should begin by questioning the very details which make the piece so outstanding. If the piecrust molding on a tilt-top table, for instance, checks out as

219. Carolean-style stool with approximately carved legs and stretchers of characteristic walnut. Its date, however, is 1920, not 1685. Note the socket tenon joint connecting the legs and stretchers; a tighter squared mortise-and-tenon joint would be the usual form for a period piece, as seen in illustration 226.

220. Mid-18th-century New Hampshire Dunlap-style high chest or highboy of maple. Photograph courtesy the Yale University Art Gallery. Mabel Brady Garvan Collection.

always having been a part of the table and not a newly applied addition, the rest of the table can be examined with the age tests and a conclusion of authenticity reached for the table as a whole. A plain early tilt-top table would be of interest and value, but a similar example with the piecrust molding intact is of even greater importance, and hence a detail of interest to the deceiver.

The wide difference in value between carved and uncarved pieces provides great incentive for the imitator to attempt to enhance the value of a piece with new carving. Flat arabesque and fret carving are often resorted to for this type of deception as they have the important advantage of allowing the face of the new ornament to retain its original surface; only the sides of the design and the background will be freshly cut. The newly cut surfaces will then be stained, waxed, rubbed and dirtied to give them the appearance of age. However, careful scrutiny should still reveal the new incisions, thus offering good proof of new work. Early chests, Bible boxes, the frieze of an oak refectory table, and the carving on Chinese Chippendale–style chairs all lend themselves to this type of carved addition.

Another opportunity for "carving up" presents itself with the knees of cabriole legs on Queen Anne and early Georgian chairs. Many knees on such chairs are known to have been carved, and this carved detail, of course, adds to the value and interest of the chairs. When such carving was intended as part of the cabinetmaker's original design, he took care to leave adequate extra stock at the knee as he carved out the leg; hence the baroque convex shell design shown in illustration 222 (leg *b*) has properly proportioned contours. The knee which has been carved out later (leg *a*) can quickly be detected because there will be little variety in the relief of the carving, since stock was not left for this purpose. The shallow carving looks inadequate at best and, to achieve even this, the leg has had to be carved down, possibly distorting the lines of the chair.

Another way the imitator will attempt to simulate age is by giving his carving a worn and rounded look all over. In studying genuine carving, however, it will be observed that although many prominent areas of the carving are rounded (from wear and handling) or even missing (again from wear and handling), the less prominent areas will remain as crisp and sharp as when originally carved. In fact, the mint-condition pieces (and hence the most desirable) have aged gracefully with their edges retained and carving intact.

Fake new inlay work on the appropriate styles of furniture (such as late 18th-century Hepplewhite and Sheraton pieces, etc.) also serves to enhance the appear-

221. Drawers of Dunlap-style historic married high chest. Note differences in upper and lower case dovetailing, drawer front thickness as well as reshaping of drawer moldings of upper case to match with those of the bottom; upper case also with through-tenon drawer dividers.

ance and value of a piece of furniture, and thus becomes another skill for the imitator to master. New wood inlays can be laid in newly cut beds in the surface of the old satinwood veneer surface, for example, and then scraped down to the general surface level. As the new glue dries, it will contract; thus the newly inlaid wood will, at times, sink below the rest of the surface. When this happens, the

222. a. *Inadequately carved knee of little projection and shallow carved detail.*
b. *Richly carved knee of properly proportioned contours.*

new inlay bed cuts are exposed and the foul play becomes obvious. A characteristic of old inlay stringing and other decorative details is the difference in surface when compared with the surrounding areas. Usually the inlays will feel higher, a subtlety caused by wood movement over time, and almost impossible to create anew.

Yet another detail, which increases the interest and thus the value of a piece, is the addition of corner brackets to a table or chair which has been without them. To add fretwork brackets to an otherwise very simple card table, for example, will increase its beauty and interest—assuming this is done carefully and in keeping with the table. Since there are many varieties of decorative bracket which can be used in several different places, constant alertness is necessary.

THE FAKING OF REPLACEMENT PARTS

Another and major fakery effort involves the introduction of new materials into pieces of furniture to replace missing or worn-out parts. This work is often essential in order to preserve a piece and to permit it to carry on its original purpose. All new materials should of course match the old in terms of exact kind, age and color. However, because such restoration work is not always identified but rather concealed with the intention of the piece maintaining its "100% originality," value and interest, the collector and buyer must be on constant guard.

A case in point might be the necessary replacement of a 17th-century oak refectory table top. To locate wide oak boards of the proper age and character with appropriate signs of wear and patina would be impossible were it not for the availability of old oak floorboards and ship deck timbers. Of course such boards have nail holes at fairly regular intervals, and these would have to be filled in or disguised in some way. An example of the problems involved in this kind of work can be seen by examining the simple American trestle table pictured in illustration 223. At first glance it appears consistently old and appropriate for its 130-year age. Closer scrutiny reveals unexplained and unlikely markings on the boards plus unreasonable, evenly spaced, filled nail holes along the edges of the boards. The history of this table is known; the table top was created in the early 20th century from fine barn floorboards which had been nailed down. Further markings are explained by the wheels of a wheelbarrow marring the surface.

Small carved and turned ornaments applied to a case, such as "split spindles" on a Boston-area press cupboard (illustration 63, page 41), frequently come loose and disappear. Many were held in place only by glue which has failed, but some were reinforced with nails. These vulnerable elements were often replaced and can be realized as such, by examining the back side and the counterpart case surface; nails should line up and there should be no signs of earlier nail holes, earlier ornament outlines on the surface, etc.

The tripod table with its circular top is a most desirable piece of furniture in today's market, and hence forgeries are common. Discarded pole screens or damaged torchères are cut down and circular tops are added. These tops sometimes come from damaged dumbwaiters, but more frequently are newly turned from old mahogany. Measuring the table top for shrinkage will usually show up new turning, since, as we have seen, wood shrinks across the grain and an old top will therefore be slightly

223. *Trestle pine board table made from barn floor boards. The boards individually measure widths of 14″, 13″ and 15″. Note the marks from the spiked wheel of a wheelbarrow.*

oval. (To achieve this proper ovoid shape, a faker will sometimes bake the new round part, thereby causing artificial shrinkage, cracking and checking.) Careful attention should also be given to the way the base and top are joined together. Clues indicating that the two pieces

have recently been joined include disturbed wood surface, new finish and modern construction methods.

Another example of careful and skillful deception is the necessary replacement of legs on a case piece, such as a highboy or a high chest. By sawing off the original legs just below where they join the vertical corner blocks or the apron, minimum disturbance of the piece takes place. Substitute legs are then dowelled in the base of the corner posts and the inner parts of this new joint are stained to aid in its disguise.

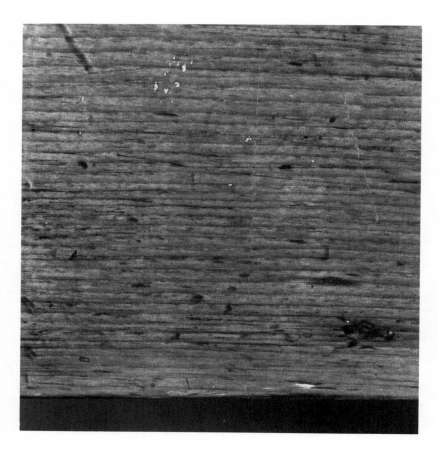

224. Close-up of the trestle table showing one of a series of suspicious nail holes. Note the common black stain surround, caused by the corroded iron nail bleeding into the wood.

Yet another opportunity for successful deception presents itself in the form of the unusually high office desk, about 38″ high from floor to writing surface, often pictured in the stories of Charles Dickens. High stools were used with these desks. With little difficulty the feet can be removed from these desks, the bottom drawer eliminated, and the projecting sides cut into feet, thereby reducing the desk to the standard and more acceptable height.

Recently, a mahogany chest of drawers came under special scrutiny due to several ink stains and unusual scratches apparent on the side wood surfaces. Further investigation revealed that this wood had once been part of a Victorian table top. Such signs of former and alien use are indeed helpful in judging the 100% originality of a piece. Careful study of the fine mid-18th-century American dressing table or lowboy shown here (illustration 225) reveals that the top is a replacement. In spite of the careful craftsmanship involved, including an appropriate edge molding, even in a photograph the wood looks different—too smooth without signs of wear, a suggestion of different color, and no patina or feeling of age.

Another example of table top alteration and replacement is seen in illustration 226. Early 18th-century gateleg tables such as this can be found with these

proportions but invariably the top and hinged leaves are each made of one piece of wood—not of several pieces as here represented. Therefore, the conclusion must be that the top is a later replacement (asssuming the base is old).

THE FAKING OF WORMHOLES

Fake wormholes have traditionally been associated with the falsifying of antique furniture. The dramatic means of achieving a wormhole effect have ranged from shotgun holes to acid and drills. It is actually quite easy to create wormholes; it is also quite easy to prove their authenticity. A soft copper wire when inserted into a wormhole will enter straight and extend deep into the hole if the wormhole is, in fact, the product of a drill. If the wire follows a meandering path it is likely that a "worm" has been there (see Chapter 13). Signs of sawdust near the entrance to the hole offer further evidence of a wormhole's authenticity; worm which is still active can be detected by tapping the wood sharply when a fine sawdust should fall from the holes.

Because wormholes are considered such a time-worn indication of antiquity, it is all the more important to be on guard against attempted fakery. Quite often one is

225. Mid-18th-century mahogany dressing table with a replacement top that lacks signs of age or use.

226. Early 18th-century gateleg table with later top and drop-leaves.

227. Woodworm channels legitimately exposed on the surface of this late 17th-century chair handrest where the wood has been worn and smoothed away by use.

presented with wood showing the meandering channels on the wood's surface as final proof that the piece is very old. But it should be remembered that the "worm" travels his devious route within the wood, only coming to the surface to depart and creating a "hole" with his exit. (These "flight holes" are never all precisely the same shape and size and are seldom exactly at right angles to the wood surface.) Sometimes exposed worm channels are legitimate due to extreme wearing away of the wood, such as on the arms of an early chair, but this is not generally the case. More typical is a 17th-century oak chest once brought to my attention whose back and bottom were constructed of old channeled wormy wood. In order to use this very old wood for replacement parts in this chest, the wood had to be cut, and thus the worm channels became exposed. "Worms" simply do not travel along the surface, so this wood could not be original to the chest. One therefore can well speculate on the original shape of the worm-riddled table leg pictured in illustration 191, page 133.

When an imitator while working a piece of old wood happens to cut through a worm channel longitudinally, rather than sectionally, and the long channel appears on the surface, he may fill it in with wax or another filler for concealment. This kind of deception is never permanently successful—the filling evenutally sinks or falls out, revealing the channel.

An ironic fact is that the informed collector prefers genuine furniture without wormholes as a sign of supposed age. (Genuine wormholes need not be old.) He realized that a piece affected by worms is being slowly depreciated in both strength and value. He also realized that eradication of the worm is extremely difficult and that the radical treatment involved may destroy the patina, further depreciating the value and beauty of the piece.

THE FAKING OF SURFACES

With lacquered and painted furniture, an antique appearance is sometimes achieved by emphasizing the cracks. These fraudulent pieces are usually made of pine. Once the surface is rubbed down, several coats of special paint are applied, the last coat being the color of the ground. The design is then drawn on and the raised portions applied. When the design has been gilded, the surface is treated with a thin coat of French polish, then topped with a coating of stiff paste or starch. The strong drawing power of the paste causes the surface of the polish to crack. The paste is then washed away and a dark-colored wax is worked into the artificial cracks thereby emphasizing them. Cracks made in this manner will be large and wide, similar in character to the cracks found in old oil paintings. They can easily be distinguished from the cracks seen on genuine lacquer or gilding which are very fine. An example of an old gilded looking glass with hairline cracks is shown in illustration 132, page 88.

The color of the interior surfaces of genuine old lacquered pieces such as the insides of cabinet doors will be brighter than outside surfaces because they are less exposed to the effects of light and atmosphere. The color of the lacquer underneath the escutcheon plate covering the keyhole has also been protected from light and should thus appear brighter if the lacquer finish is indeed old.

On a genuine piece of gilt furniture, such as a table, it will be noticed that the portions of the table that face upwards will be dark in comparison with those parts that face downwards. This is due to dust having collected on the upturned part and slowly darkened the surface of the gilding. This sullying effect of dust can be recognized on an old gilt picture frame; if the frame has always been hung in the same position, the bottom upturned side will be perceptibly darker than the inside top of the frame which faces downward. This darkening effect of dust, although more accentuated on original gilt pieces of the early 18th century, is also discernible on pieces gilded as recently as 25 or 30 years ago. This observation, therefore, can only be used as a test for gilding of quite recent manufacture. The faker does not often imitate this undoubted but subtle sign of a certain age.

Gold does not tarnish but it does mellow with accumulated dust and dirt. To tone down the brightness of recently applied gold, the imitator uses a wash of stain over the gilt surface. For detection, this surface can be gently wiped, thus removing the stain and exposing the bright gilding beneath. It will take two or three years for the surface to become sufficiently hard to resist this test.

The accessories of a piece of fake furniture also require "work." Stories of burying brasses in the ground to achieve an old look and dipping them in acids and abrading them with flails to create the impression of wear contain much truth. Many methods were, and still are, tried and used—the desired final result being for brasses and hinges to appear worn, old and original to the piece. Old nails can be fabricated in the old hand-forged way and then "aged" by some of the above suggested methods. Alternatively, Victorian cut-nails can simply be hammered, thereby simulating the handwork of the earlier nails. The best defense against fake accessories is to seize all opportunities for studying genuine hardware.

CAUTIONS FOR COLLECTORS

Fascinating deeds of fakery can be discussed ad infinitum, but the main purpose here is to instill caution. Late period sideboards, for example, become more desirable (and hence profitable) when today's imitator cuts off the round legs and fixes tapered square legs onto the stumps. In purchasing a sideboard, therefore, the collector should always examine the legs where they join the case to ensure that this substitution has not been carried out. Another trick is to take the heavy legs of an Empire-style dining-room table and turn them down on a lathe into legs of earlier styles, thereby enhancing the current value of the table.

The shrewd collector should always pay special heed to the tops of tall clocks, the tops of highboys, and other remote and secondary areas to which the imitator is likely to have paid the least attention. It is almost impossible to add, subtract or change any furniture element without having to disguise such alterations with staining or refinishing. Examine furniture in natural daylight; in artificial light it is very difficult to perceive gradations of color which in daylight can easily be observed. The variation in wood color between old and new parts and the differences in their surface condition, and efforts of the imitator to hide restored parts with stain, will also become apparent in natural light. It should be realized that new wood tends to fade more than the older wood surrounding it; thus, a new wood replacement or repair will appear lighter unless it initially has been stained darker to compensate for this greater fading. Questionable stained and dirtied wax can be scratched or removed with a fingernail (or even rubbed off a furniture surface) and its presence is a sure sign of a faked surface.

Careful inspection of drawers is another way to guard against fakes. The interiors of early drawers and cabinets are surprisingly clean and fresh looking. It is impossible for the imitator to reproduce this appearance. Attempts are made to do so, however, by staining with aniline dyes, painting the interiors in oil colors (usually green or brown) or "wallpapering" the drawers with old newspapers or blue paper, this having been the fashion at one time. Another attempt is the practice of spilling ink inside the drawers, particularly those of a chest of drawers or a desk.

The wise collector will always exercise care when presented with a provenance (history of ownership) for a piece of furniture. All pieces of antique furniture must have histories but these should be carefully validated. The antique dealer's familiar quote, "Oh, I bought this chair from a wonderful little old lady who inherited it from her grandmother," may indeed be appealing and sell chairs, but it must be recognized for what it is—a sales pitch.

Unscrupulous antique dealers have been known to show great dishonesty concerning provenance. Fine pieces are sometimes "planted" in a country house implying that they have been in the family's possession for a

228. *Top of back side of highboy. A good place to look for signs of deception: consistent nail history, uniform natural oxidized color of backboards, which are usually laid* horizontally and nailed to the case side rabbet joints, and often the top board extends below the cornice molding on a bonnet-top piece.

number of years. Or it will be falsely claimed that a piece from a certain collection was purchased at a given auction. Many times these facts can be checked if the effort is made.

Dealers and collectors alike are impressed with cabinetmakers' labels found on old pieces of furniture. Such labels make a piece of furniture much more interesting in that more of its history can be learned. And if a certain cabinetmaker's work is especially fine and desirable, the piece becomes more valuable as the identified product of his work. Here shown is the only known labeled piece of furniture made by Edmund Townsend of Newport. Needless to say, however, a label may not be genuine and thus should be held in suspicion at all times. Labels can be very simple things to reproduce given the knowledge of old techniques and the proper old tools, and imitators have become most successful in this regard.

One practice for faking labels is to clip a cabinetmaker's advertisement from an old newspaper or city directory and paste it to a piece of old furniture. The letterhead of an old bill will serve the same purpose. This type of faking can be recognized by the lack of decorative borders and the difference in typography. Labels made from newspaper advertisements have distinctively small type; were such a "label" carefully moistened and lifted, printing would be revealed on the back, showing that it is not a genuine label as they were never printed on the back. (However, one must never remove a label from a piece of furniture because the credibility would be lost.) Thrilling as it would be to discover an original label, one would be foolish to set great store by such a discovery. (For more about labels see Chapter 16.)

Unless the maker of spurious furniture limits himself to trying to produce an exact replica of a good old piece, he will invariably commit an error in the proportion or ornamentation of his ware. Torn between the desire to produce a passable antique and the desire to increase its selling potential, he may make the dimensions smaller to better suit today's smaller rooms, or he may be tempted to produce a "unique" or "rare" piece of furniture. Errors of dimension and proportion may be coupled with misuse of decoration on pieces of a given style. By careful

230. *Detail, Edmund Townsend paper label. Photograph courtesy the Museum of Fine Arts, Boston.*

229. *Bureau table, mahogany, 1765–1775, made by Edmund Townsend (1736–1811). A fine example of Newport design and craftsmanship, this piece is uniquely documented with an original label on the upper side of the top drawer bottom (see detail, illustration 230). Note the typical single-board top; a period case top or sides were never constructed with multiple narrow boards.*

study of genuine pieces, the collector can become familiar with the general characteristics peculiar to each period. (A case in point would be the seat of a mid-18th-century mahogany side chair whose seat always appears—and should appear—too big when one looks straight down on it.)

It must be pointed out that the subtleties of old furniture can be reproduced by a man who knows his business as an impostor—a skillful cabinetmaker using genuine pieces as models and wood of the proper kind and age. There have been some famous practitioners, known by name, of this type of deceit who have known as much about old furniture as the museum people and other professionals who finally judged their creations.

Such situations lead to fascinating battles of wits between experts. In the case of a really good faked piece of furniture, the novice has no chance whatsoever of making a true identification. As proof of this, we conclude our discussion with two sets of comparative detail photographs of two "Philadelphia Chippendale-style" chairs, one of which has only recently been deemed quite modern despite excellent craftsmanship, good faking and a genuine Randolph label glued to the inside rear seat rail. The details reproduced here represent areas where the deception is *not* convincing. As one focuses on these details, however, the skills and abilities represented in the falsely old chair must be admired.

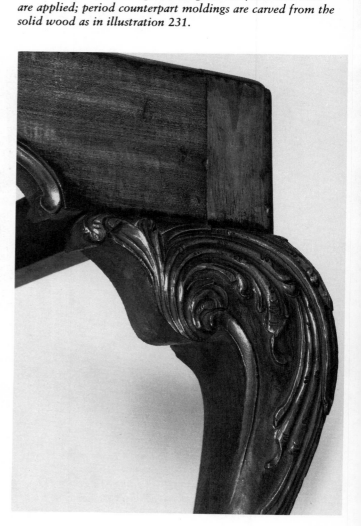

232. *Knee bracket of Philadelphia Chippendale-style chair of questionable age: the carving is smooth, careful and "clean" on the secondary surfaces without the characteristic exuberant and impatient signs of hand craftsmanship. The C-scroll carved lower edge moldings on the front seat rails are applied; period counterpart moldings are carved from the solid wood as in illustration 231.*

231. *Knee bracket of Philadelphia 18th-century chair; underside hand-tooling marks are clearly visible and can be easily felt on the secondary wood surfaces.*

233. *Old cornerblock, 18th-century Philadelphia Chippendale-style chair. Hand-planed marks can be seen on the cornerblock and on the inside seat rail. The smoky look of time is present (recall our discussions of naturally oxidized secondary surfaces) and signs of wear can be found on the chair stile and seat rail edge.*

234. *New stained pine cornerblock, Philadelphia Chippendale-style chair. Hand-planed marks can be found. An attempt has been made to suggest oxidation over time on the interior surface, including "dirt" placed in the corners of the cornerblock. There are no signs of wear. The Benjamin Randolph label is genuine, however.*

Chapter 16

Conclusions

WHILE ALL OF THESE thoughts may be useful, of course no proven single detail or proven single test for age is adequate for proper definition of the piece. Even a collection of "check points" will not necessarily provide the whole story; it simply helps. The true connoisseur is always skeptical. Sometimes evidence may be distorted, accidentally, deliberately or simply by such events as stripping, regilding, repolishing or repairing. There are also exceptions to all rules—the sides of a chest may not be planed smooth, for example, drawer pulls may never have been put on a chest, and no two chairs will ever be exactly alike. Thus the study of antique furniture is never-ending. With constant observation and study, increasing familiarity leads to a developed instinct for what is and what is not old. This instinct is a composite of formal lessons, observation, experience, good eyes and common sense.

Collecting old furniture is the source of much pleasure, interest and challenge to the collector. There is the pleasure of living with one's collection, a constant source of satisfaction and education. There is the pleasure of realizing that a truly fine piece of furniture will retain its aesthetic appeal as long as civilization as we know it continues. There is pleasure in the recognition that fine rare pieces will become increasingly scarce over the years, thereby rising in monetary value.

Successful collecting requires the application of all previous study, experience and training to the object under review, thus giving one the assurance to know what to look for and where to look. Perhaps the best way to approach a piece of furniture is to develop a simple set of priorities. Probably anyone's first reaction when confronted with an unknown piece will be to try to identify its style, a subject that is beyond the scope of this text. With a tentative style dating, using criteria of size (scale and silhouette), material, decorative details and color, one then moves in closer to consider whether the piece is of the period when that style was prevalent, or whether it is a later piece in that style. Certain age characteristics will be particularly evident, and these will be the concentration, always recognizing that no detail can be relied upon in isolation. In fact, as one examines various parts of a piece, one should be on the alert for details consistent to age or contrary-to-age. If one finds many consistent details as evidence of age (or not) one can advance a step closer to drawing a conclusion. Understanding visible repairs and damages and their causes will help, and all holes or unusual construction details should be logical. Then, developed and disciplined intuition will hopefully reinforce one's findings. If all is still right, information about the ownership history of the piece (its provenance) will help to confirm conclusions, and the

235. *Eighteenth-century American high chest of drawers which has never had door pulls attached.*

established market price for the piece will provide the final respect.

Careful study of dates on which new designs, decorative motifs and material were introduced is most important. Anachronisms can often be discovered when examining a suspect piece, thereby building support for its "not right" status. (The basic guide for establishing the date of a piece of furniture with characteristic features of more than one style is to use the date of the latest style detail—a cabinetmaker could work with earlier details but not those yet to be created.) It is also important to establish whether a form of furniture was popular at a particular time or even made then at all. For example, sideboards simply were not made much before

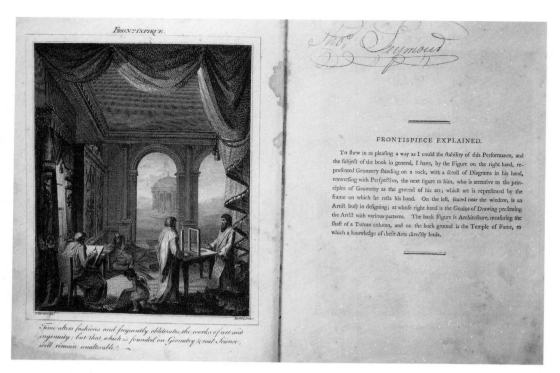

236. *Frontispiece from* The Cabinet-Maker and Upholsterer's Drawing-Book *in 3 parts, 1793, by Thomas Sheraton, London (1791–1793). This pattern book with the signature of Thomas Seymour on the Explanatory Leaf of the Frontispiece is the only known example of a pattern book bearing the signature of an American cabinetmaker.*

Seymour presumably acquired the book after 1793 while working in Boston; in 1800, Thomas became associated with his father, John Seymour, who was an outstanding cabinetmaker in Boston after the Revolution. Photograph courtesy the Museum of Fine Arts, Boston.

237. *The mid-18th-century decorative London trade card of case- and cabinetmaker John Folgham, 8⅝″ by 6¼″. Such a label establishes the furniture maker's address and occupation, and when the card includes engravings of furniture, the style and quality of his work can be suggested. From Sir Ambrose Heal:* The London Furniture Makers, 1660–1840, *New York: Dover Publications, Inc., 1972.*

168 · **What Happens to Furniture with Time**

1780 in America or in England. Cabinets for the display of china were rarely made before 1715. The forger is tempted to compensate for such deficiencies.

There are several important sources of information for dating the details of historic furniture. For example, 18th-century English style motifs can be documented in period publications, the surviving cabinetmakers' illustrated and dated records of furniture designs—catalogs, advertisements and directories. Counterpart American historic furniture-maker daybooks, etc., are being discovered and made available for study; the Winterthur Museum Library is especially important for reference material in this regard. Many large English houses are also known to have been furnished at certain dates and in some cases this documented original furniture remains in place today serving as an excellent reference source. Dyrham Park in Gloucestershire, England, is a fine example of this, likewise the Gardner-Pingree House, Salem, Massachusetts.

Advertisements and trade cards of cabinetmakers and shopkeepers, travel diaries, family letters, probate court household inventories, and memoirs are interesting and useful sources for documentation. Early paintings and engravings in which furniture appears are another excellent source as the piece is visible and often shown in color. John Singleton Copley's portraits (see illustration 95, page 65) are well endowed with 18th-century furniture including good detail of the materials and techniques used to cover chairs, sofas and other pieces of the time.

Evidence of date is sometimes found in printed matter glued to the piece, such as an original label of a cabinetmaker. If any record of that cabinetmaker can be found from early newspaper advertisements, directories, court entries, etc., it may be possible to establish the date of his working career. Such research may ascertain a label to be that of a later repairer whose dates may be established in a similar way or it may lead to the realization that a father and son, both cabinetmakers,

238. English dressing case circa 1800 with label of Dobson, Hardwareman *behind inner lid (see illustration 239).*

239. English dressing case showing label. Information about "Hardwareman Dobson" and this example of his work could likely be discovered with research into the historic records of London cabinetmaking.

Conclusions · 169

240. *Panel of characteristic Samuel McIntire rich carving as found on his mahogany chest-on-chest, likely made for Elizabeth Derby of Salem, Massachusetts, in 1796. Photograph courtesy the Museum of Fine Arts, Boston.*

had the same name and used the same label, thereby spreading the likely date range of the piece under consideration.

Rare but exciting documentary evidence for dating a piece of furniture is found in a dated bill rendered by a cabinetmaker. The furniture must be sufficiently described to connect the bill and extant piece. Such bills and documented furniture exist from the workshop of Duncan Phyfe in New York City. Harewood House in Yorkshire, England, has many bills concerning purchases of furniture for the house from the shop of Thomas Chippendale.

Dates of American furniture are sometimes suggested by the number of stars inlaid or painted on a piece. The implication here is that the number of stars indicates the number of states in the Union at the time it was made and decorated. Sometimes this correlation holds true.

Dating furniture is also done by attribution; i.e., if several pieces are found to have exactly the same characteristics, cabinetmaking designs and ornamental details, and if the maker of one of them is known, all of the pieces may be attributed to that maker, thereby approximating the date of them all. The carved details of Samuel McIntire of Salem, Massachusetts—his cornucopia, basket of fruit and flowers, sheaf of wheat, and alternating blocks of flutes and rosette borders—are so well known and copied (both now and in the past) that it is uncertain and speculative to justify attribution on the basis of those details alone. In cases of attribution, caution must always be exercised.

Fashion also plays a role in collecting old furniture and, indeed, what is most fashionable dictates and realizes the highest prices. Thus the wise collector should recognize that provided a piece is appealing and a good example of its period style, truly old in itself, and in good condition, the absence of current popularity (which inflates its price) can be an advantage. Furthermore, an unfashionable piece at a low price is not likely to be faked.

Study of the marketplace for antique furniture should clarify for the collector and student alike the fact that a particularly high price for an object is no guarantee of its authenticity. At the same time usually only a dealer in stolen goods can afford to sell below market value. Forgeries are usually offered at a price sufficiently below market value to tempt the thoughtless buyer, but not so low as to be immediately suspect.

With so many details to examine and consider, perhaps it should go without saying that it is important to take one's time before reaching conclusions. Sit down and spend twenty minutes simply looking at the piece—how much you will glean in minute details and clues to its age! Explore the back side and underside with even greater fastidiousness. Examination of the piece in daylight out-of-doors will also reveal small details which are not easily discerned in lesser light. Physically lift the piece of furniture; an 18th-century American Chippendale-style chair should be heavy, since it is likely to be made of thick, heavy San Domingan mahogany. In any important decision it is wise to confirm your conclusions with a qualified and recognized authority on antique furniture.

A most valuable and wonderful way for learning about, understanding and appreciating the skills of the furniture cabinetmaker and craftsman is time actually spent in his workshop. Knowledge of methods, tools and materials used by furniture craftsmen, old and contemporary, aids the collector in protecting himself against forgeries. More important, however, is the experience of watching such an expert craftsman and discussing his work with him. Respect and fascination for his capabilities, skills and pride evolve, never to be forgotten.

241. Back side of a looking-glass frame providing information on construction, on replacement details or missing parts, and on where and how repairs have been made. Note the cresting glueblock supports to minimize warpage.

GLOSSARY

A

Acanthus
A form of ornament, based on the leaves of the acanthus plant, used for the enrichment of moldings and surfaces: the carved knees of chairs and tables, and the arms and cresting of chairs.

Adze
A type of axe with the cutting edge at right angles to the handle. Horizontal rather than vertical strokes are used to work the adze.

Annual Rings
Concentric alternating light and dark areas, when a tree is viewd in cross section, are called annual or growth rings. A new ring appears each year representing a year's growth. The older annual rings, in the center (so-called heartwood), are usually darker and no longer function as channels of growth. The younger rings, closest to the edge (sapwood), are lighter and transport the nutrients upwards.

Apron
A shaped horizontal piece of wood below the seat rail of a chair or the frame of a case piece or table, extending between the legs, which is usually ornamented with shaping, carving or piercing; also called the "skirt."

Astragal
A small half-round or convex bead molding.

B

Bail
A curving pull handle, often of brass, hanging from metal bolts and backed by a metal plate. As of about 1700, it was used on drawer fronts.

Banding
A narrow edging or border of veneer around the fronts of drawers, etc.; a contrasting band of inlay.

Banisters
The upright turned members in a chair back or a staircase balustrade.

Bellflower
A classical style motif; flower bud of three to five narrow pointed petals, usually inlaid into veneered wood.

Bevel
A sloping edge of various angles applied to wood or glass or metal. (See Chamfer.)

Birdcage
A construction device which allows the top of a tripod table to revolve when horizontal and to be tipped up when not in use. It consists of two squares of wood connected by small turned pillars, thus resembling a birdcage. The lower square is pierced by a hole through which the pedestal is fixed by means of a wedge. The upper part is hinged to the table top by two long bearers, screwed to the underside.

Blind tracery
Tracery carved upon a solid wooden surface, characteristic of Gothic tracery.

Block front
The front of a chest of drawers, secretary or desk having different planes on its surface—the center section or side sections project or are recessed to achieve a constrast or blocked front. This form seems to be peculiarly American, a baroque expression dating from the period of 1760–1780, and is associated with the work of the Townsend-Goddard School in Newport.

Bole
A colored claylike substance (red, yellow, blue, gray) applied over carved wood looking-glass or picture frames, which is finely grained and creates a smooth ground for gilding. The tone of the gilding is made warmer or cooler depending on the color of the bole ground, which reflects through the gold.

Bombé
The outward swelling or convex surface found on cabinets and commodes; a fashion originating in Italy and Holland which was reflected in the mid-18th-century Boston-area chests of drawers and desk-and-bookcases made by cabinetmakers like John Cogswell.

Bonnet top
The curved hooded broken-arch/scroll pediment topping tall case furniture.

Boss
A round or oval-shaped applied wooden ornament, often used with applied split spindles and drops on 17th-century American case pieces and frequently painted black to suggest ebony wood.

Boulle work (Premier work)
The practice of inlaying brass into wood or tortoiseshell; this form of marquetry was introduced by André-Charles Boulle (1642–1732), a French cabinetmaker under the patronage of Louis XIV.

Bracket foot
A foot shaped like a straight bracket, supporting chests of drawers and other case pieces, and extending a short way in both directions from the corner of the base.

Bun foot
A foot in the form of a bunlike flattened sphere, used on chairs, tables, stands and chests, which came into general use during the latter part of the 17th century.

Burl
An abnormal wartlike protruding growth on the trunk or branches of a tree. Examined closely, it may consist of a great mass of "eyes" or dormant buds. When sliced as a veneer it reveals beautiful figure, which was used frequently by late 17th-century cabinetmakers working in the William and Mary style.

C

C-scroll
An ornamental scroll, in the shape of the letter C, often used in carved enrichment; its name derives from the Greek word cyma.

Cabinetmaker
The highly skilled and specialized maker of furniture, whose craft was created and developed by the technique of veneering, introduced into England during the second half of the 17th century. (Compare with the craft of the joiner.) The cabinetmaker became identified with fine furniture during the 18th century, and cabinetmaking has since become a generic term for the making of furniture.

Cabochon
Carved decorative detail, resembling a cartouche, sometimes carved on the knees of cabriole legs during the mid-18th century. Its smooth raised round or elliptical center was often surrounded by acanthus leafage.

Cabriole leg
A leg consisting of two curves, the upper part (the shoulder or knee) convex, and the lower part, above the shaped foot, concave.

Caddy (Tea caddy)
A small box or chest often decorated with wood veneers and inlay, etc., used for keeping tea, an expensive commodity in the 17th and 18th centuries. The word caddy is a corruption of catti (kati), a weight used in the East, equal to just over a pound.

Cant
A form of chamfer or bevel, frequently used in reference to the front corners of case pieces of furniture.

Carpenter
The carpenter has been concerned with structural woodwork in building, such as timber-framed roofs, since medieval times. From his craft the joiner's craft evolved.

Cartouche
A rococo decoration based on the scroll with an oval shape and curled and rolled-over edges, used frequently on mid-18th-century mahogany furniture. In Philadelphia, free-standing carved cartouches were used as the center finials for tall case pieces.

Carver
Throughout furniture history the wood carver has generally worked in partnership with furniture makers, joiners or others who were responsible for making a complete object. The carver's job was to embellish the piece in question. During the late 17th century and throughout the 18th century the carver and gilder had great prominence, becoming responsible for the carving and gilding of such ornate articles as looking-glass frames, console tables, candelabra and girandoles.

Caul
A stout piece of wood, slightly convex on the underside and a little larger than the panel of veneer being glued. The caul was heated and then clamped to the newly glued veneer surface for support, the heat passing through the veneers and liquefying the glue previously applied. The convex surface ensured that pressure began at the center and continued to the edges. The caul would be kept tightly in place until the glue was dry.

Chamfer
A flat surface formed by planing or flattening the angle made where two surfaces meet. (See *Bevel*.)

Chip carving
Simple and shallow form of carving used to decorate wooden surfaces in the 13th, 14th and 15th centuries. The patterns, which were usually geometrical, were first set out with compasses and then carefully chipped out with chisels and gouges, probably by the joiner who made the chest. Chip carving continued through the 16th and early 17th centuries.

Cock-bead
A continuous bead molding based on a semicircular section, which projected beyond an edge or surface. It was often used in the mid-18th century around drawer fronts.

Concertina action
A construction device often used for mid-18th-century card tables with folding tops. When the moveable legs of such tables were pulled out, the horizontal hinged frame to which they were attached straightened out and served as a support for the opened top. When the table was closed, this framing folded back like a concertina.

Contre-partie boulle
Brass groundwork with tortoiseshell inlay, counterpart match of premier boulle.

Cresting
The carved decoration atop the crest rail of a chair or settee or the back of a daybed.

Cross-banding
Border bands of veneer in which the grain runs across the band. This decorative banding was characteristic of late 17th- and early 18th-century veneered case furniture.

Cross-grain molding
A molding with the grain of the wood running across its width and not along its length. Cross-grained moldings were a characteristic feature of walnut furniture in the late 17th century and early part of the 18th century.

Crotch
The place in a tree where the main trunk (or large branch) forks to produce two smaller branches. Crotch-figure wood is obtained from wood directly below the bifurcation.

D

Diaper
Decoration consisting of repetitions of small repeats, sometimes flower sprigs, geometric lozenges, etc., even dots (thus polkadots), forming an allover pattern on a surface. This form of repeating pattern is used in marquetry, and frequently for upholstery textile designs.

Drop-leaf
A table with hinged leaves that can be raised to enlarge it. Supports for the leaves are either legs or other supports swung into position. Such tables include butterfly tables, corner tables, gateleg tables and so-called Pembroke tables.

E

Ébénistes
Members of the French guild who faced the surfaces of their furniture with veneers of precious wood, and furniture treated in this way was confined to chests of drawers, desks and tables. The term ébéniste goes back to the second half of the 17th century when furniture veneered with ebony became fashionable with well-to-do people. Later in the 18th century, when more colorful woods were largely substituted for ebony, men so engaged still called themselves ébénistes.

Escutcheon
Ornamental keyhole plate, usually brass, placed over and surrounding the keyhole for the lock.

F

Facing
A term in furniture construction meaning a thin covering of wood, such as mahogany, not necessarily a veneer, upon a ground of secondary wood.

Figure
The natural decorative marking or pattern seen on the surface of cut wood caused by variations of light reflectivity from the different sizes, shapes, angles and colors of cells. This pattern is not the grain of the wood but rather its figure. Figure results from the interaction of several features present in the wood—including the presence or absence of growth rings, the prominence of and abundance of vascular rays, and local variations in color due to uneven deposition of coloring substances in wood. Figure can be emphasized or deemphasized by the way the log is cut, a tangentially cut board having very different figure than were it radially cut, for example.

Finial
Carved wood or brass terminal ornament projecting upward from the cornice or pediment from the cornice or pediment of a case piece (such as a high chest or clock case). Finials also terminate the tops of chair stiles.

Flitch
A section of log which has been sawn into a bundle of consecutive sheets of veneer.

Fluting
Shallow concave grooves on a surface are called flutes, and flutes used in vertical parallel series are known as fluting—such as the fluting on a column or a chair leg. Fluting was a decorative detail used in ancient classical architecture on columns and pilasters and was used for furniture parts during the late 18th-century classical-revival style. Good flutes are close together and deep with a sharply scooped curve for the ending; the ridge between the flutes is called a fillet.

French foot
A bracket foot which splays outward as it nears the floor.

French polish
A finish introduced and used extensively in the 19th century in which a finish is produced by treating the surface of the wood

with shellac in spirit, using a pad in continuous movement for the difficult application. The skillful process of building up thin layers of shellac provides a lustrous finish which is relatively easy to rebuild if it becomes marred.

G

Gadroon
A carved ornamental molding—angled, rounded alternating convex and concave sections. This detail was particularly popular on furniture in New York during the mid-18th century.

Gateleg
A form of drop-leaf table with swinging leaf supports that are legs joined to the main frame of the table by upper and lower stretchers which make a gate. These swinging supports were used for gateleg tables in the late 17th century and early 18th century.

Gesso
A composition of a white material (usually gypsum or whiting), linseed oil and glue. It was used either as a ground for paintings or as a smooth surface treatment for plain or carved wood upon which was laid a metallic leaf such as gold or paint.

Gilding
The decoration of surfaces with applied gold leaf or gold dust. The practice of gilding furniture, particularly the stands of cabinets, became fashionable in the time of Charles II in England.

Girandole
A circular convex looking glass with candle brackets as part of the frame.

Gouge
A hollow chisel used by cabinetmakers and carvers.

Gouge work
The name given to gouge carving, a rudimentary form of surface decoration achieved by scooping out repeating spaced shallow depressions with a gouge. The resulting pattern was a kind of fluting, used during the late 16th and 17th centuries.

Grain
Wood grain refers to the direction or orientation of wood cells, particularly the longitudinal fibrous elements.

Graining
The highly skilled imitation of the color and wood figure, the wood surface design/pattern of a given cut board surface grain of a costly wood, achieved with paint on the surface of a less interesting and expensive wood. This was first done in England at the end of the 16th century for the imitation of oak and walnut.

H

Hardwoods
Woods supplied from broadleaved trees, belonging to the botanical group Angiosperms.

Hasp
Hinged part of a hinge lock such as the elaborate iron locks found on 15th-century European chests.

Herringbone
Pattern in the form of herringbone (alternately slanting grain) was used as inlay banding on early 18th-century walnut veneered furniture.

Hinge
A folding metal joint by which doors, lids, etc., swing on a pivot center.

I

Inlay
A method of decorating a solid wood surface, by which decorative cuts are made into the wooden ground and these cuts or grooves are filled with other materials, either woods of different colors or metal, ivory or mother-of-pearl.

Intarsia (or Tarsia)
A term of Renaissance Italy origin to describe inlay patterns, especially of wood. This work, often of a geometric or pictorial nature, was in the form of panels for walls or incorporated into furniture.

J

Japanning
European and Ameican imitation of Oriental lacquer work, using layers of paint and varnish with raised plaster Chinoiserie designs. This technique was fashionable in late 17th-century England and America. A book of instructions, *A Treatise of Japanning and Varnishing* by Stalker and Parker, was published in 1688 in London.

Joiner
The craft of the joiner, or "joyner," evolved from carpentry. The joiner handled woodwork that was smaller in scale than structural woodwork, which was the carpenter's province, and he developed a careful and exacting technique, based upon firmness and accuracy, in the making of mortise-and-tenon joints plus skill in smoothing solid wood surfaces.

Joinery
The technique of joining together pieces of solid wood.

K

Knee
The upper convex curve or bulge of a cabriole leg.

Kneehole
The opening between the two banks of drawers constructed for certain desks, such as pedestal desks, allowing room for the sitter's knees.

Knot
Cross section of a branch or limb at the point where a limb emerges from a tree trunk.

L

Lathe
A machine for shaping turned parts which holds the revolving wood during applications of the chisel cutting edge.

Linenfold panel (or Parchment panel)
A form of ornament used on wall panelling and the panels of chests and on chair backs during the early 16th century, consisting of vertical molding terminating in carved folds. The design may have originally been suggested by folded linen or by scrolls of parchment. It was of Continental origin, probably from Flanders, and came to England at the end of the 15th century.

Lopers
An English term for the sliding rails or slides which pull out from the frame of a slant-front desk to support the open hinged lid.

M

Masterpiece
Piece of work by which a journeyman craftsman gained the recognized rank of "master" craftsman from his guild.

Menuisier
Woodworker in solid wood ornamented with carving. Pieces of furniture thus produced were cupboards, side tables (consoles), chairs and beds.

Mirror
The word mirror first meant a hand mirror or any reflecting surface, and early mirrors, dating back to ancient history in China and Egypt, were of polished metal. When glass was coated with amalgam of mercury, the term looking glass, or glass, replaced mirror. It was not until the late 19th century that the word mirror came back into general use, and was applied to all forms of looking glasses.

Molding
A continuous decorative band projection or incision, curved or faceted in section, or with combined curves and facets.

Mortise
Oblong or square hole or slot cut by a chisel made for that purpose, which is designed to receive a counterpart projecting piece of wood called a tenon to form a joint, the so-called mortise-and-tenon joint.

N

Nulling
A form of carved decoration of alternating concave and convex flutes, sometimes described as gadrooning, used on the flat or molded edges of tables and cabinet stands, etc., in the 17th and 18th centuries.

O

Ogee
The common name for the molding known in classical architecture as cyma recta. In section it has a double curve, concave above and convex below.

Ogee reversed
The common name for the molding in classical architecture known as cyma reversa. In section it has a double curve, convex above, concave below. The 18th-century ogee bracket foot is in fact a reverse ogee curve.

Ormolu
An alloy of copper, zinc and tin (bronze) which is gilded and used for decorative mounts on furniture. Its use is associated chiefly with the ornate furniture made in France during the 18th century, and in France these mounts are described as bronze doré (gilded bronze).

Overcuts
Hand-saw overcuts occur in the process of cutting dovetail joints, often visible in corners of 18th-century drawer interiors.

Ovolo
A wide convex molding, used both for architecture and cabinet making, which is quarter-round in section, being a quadrant of a circle.

P

Panel
A sunken or raised surface, framed by the grooved stiles and rails of a door, or the front or lid of a chest.

Parcel gilt
Partly gilded. Carved mahogany mid-18th-century looking-glass frames, for example, often have parts picked out (highlighted) with gilding, hence the frame is parcel gilt.

Pediment
An architectural term for a triangular or curved low gable above the upper member of a classical cornice. This form was used on top of case pieces of furniture in many shapes: triangular/segmental, broken-triangular, scroll, broken-scroll/swan's neck, etc.; some were pierced.

Pendant
A term that applies to a variety of furniture ornaments all of which hang down or drop.

Pietra-Dura
A form of ornamental mosaic work introduced in 16th-century Renaissance Italy, whereby hard stones, such as agate, lapis lazuli, jasper and fragments of precious marbles, were inlaid into a surface and highly polished. Table tops of importance and decorative cabinets of the period were so ornamented, plus 19th-century revivals.

Pilaster
A vertical architectural detail, rectangular in section, projecting slightly from the surface though attached, and reproducing the characteristic proportions of a base, column and capital in one of the orders of architecture. Pilasters were an important feature of 18th-century cabinetwork.

Pollard oak (also walnut, poplar, willow and elm)
Wood with a wavy grain, which is supplied from trees that have been "topped" and their growth arrested. Pollarding involves the removal of the crown or top branches of a tree, leaving the main stem intact.

Q

Quadrant
Metal device, usually brass, of quarter-circle shape used to support the open writing surface of some fall-front desks constructed in the late 18th/early 19th century.

R

Rail
The horizontal member(s) in the frame of a case piece or panelling. The horizontal members of a table or chair frame are also known as rails.

Rebate (or Rabbet)
A continuous rectangular channel or sinking, cut along the edge of a piece of wood or framework.

Reeding
The decoration of a surface by a series of parallel convex half-round moldings of equal width. Sheraton in his 1803 *Cabinet Dictionary* speaks of reeding as a mode by which table legs, bed pillars, etc., are ornamented, and as one of the most substantial kinds of ornament yet adopted. "It is much preferable to fluting or cabling in point of strength; and in look, much superior to the latter; and almost the only ornament that has escaped the notice of the ancients, as I do not recollect any instance of reeding in any part of ancient architecture. When reeding is introduced on flat surfaces, there ought always to be 3, 5, 7, and so on, and the odd one should be in the center."

RH factor
Relative humidity factor. The amount of moisture actually in the air at a specific temperature divided by (relative to) the maximum amount of moisture the air can hold at that temperature expressed as a percentage. The warmer the air, the more moisture it can hold. Therefore if cold air is heated and no additional moisture is added, the relative humidity will drop. The single most important factor for wood movement is the relative humidity (RH).

Rococo
The word rococo derives from the French word *rocaille* which means "rock work," a term used originally to describe the artificial grottos and fountains in the gardens of Versailles. The rococo style developed in France during the early part of the Louis XV Period and it reached England in the mid-18th century, influencing Thomas Chippendale and his contemporaries. The style was exuberant, light, graceful and asymmetrical, intermingling ornamental forms of foliage, shells, scrolls and acanthus leaves.

Rottenstone
Soft, finely powdered stone used with oil to polish wood furniture surfaces.

S

S-scroll
Ornamental detail, often carved, in an S-shape, based on the cyma recta and cyma reversa curves of ancient classical architecture.

Scratch carving
The simplest form of incised carving, consisting of single lines scratched in the surface of woodwork with a V-chisel. Such carving is found on early 17th-century pieces.

Scratch stock
A simple tool for working moldings, inlays, etc., in which an adjustable cutter of thin steel is held between two pieces of wood screwed together and notched at one end. Scraping or scratching action across the wood cuts the molding, and depth is controlled by the top of the notch bearing down on the surface of the wood.

Serpentine front
A convex curve flanked by two concave curves, used on the fronts of chests of drawers, commodes, sideboards, etc.; first appeared in the mid-18th century.

Slip seat
A separate upholstered wood frame seat which lets into the primary wood rails of the chair seat.

Splat
The central shaped vertical member, often pierced and carved, of an open chair back, below the crest rail and flanked by the stiles.

Splay
An outward curved shape. A French bracket foot is a form of splayed foot.

Split spindles
Vertically halved spindles (balusters and banisters) lightly glued together, turned and then separated and applied as decoration to 17th-century oak case furniture. Split spindles are also used for the backs of banister-back chairs, with the smooth/flat side of the split banisters to the sitter's back.

Stiles
The vertical members in the panel frame of a door or case piece into which the horizontal members (rails) are fitted. The vertical members of a chair back are also called stiles.

Stop-fluting
Flutes where channels are partially filled with a counterpart convex device such as continuous bead or brass reed.

Strapwork
A form of decoration used on late 16th- and 17th-century furniture consisting of applied flat interlacing carved bands (or straps). Free-standing pierced and carved strapwork back splats are characteristic of chairs in the 18th-century Chippendale style.

Stretcher
Horizontal rails which connect the legs of stools, chairs, tables, and stands for chests, providing a strengthening function. In the late 17th century the stretcher also became a decorative feature for chairs and tables. Although it survived during the 18th century, its use was discontinued by fashionable cabinet-makers towards the end of that century.

Stringing
Narrow inlay strips (strings) of contrasting colored wood.

Woods frequently used for stringing were holly, satinwood, boxwood and ebony.

Style
Description of the design and ornamental details characteristic of the furniture of any given time, period, place, person or group. A style may be interpreted in reflective ways in other countries or times.

Swage block
An iron block containing holes and grooves of various sizes used for heading bolts and shaping objects not easily worked on an anvil.

T

Tambour
Flexible sliding panel doors, usually horizontal, which move in a grooved track, made of canvas with applied half-round turned members (reeds). (These run in a groove and may follow any shape.) This detail was favored in Louis XVI work and exploited by the Seymour cabinetmakers of Boston.

Template (templet)
A flat pattern outline cut out of thin wood or card for each part to be joined to form a piece of furniture. For a Queen Anne chair, there would be templates for front and back legs, the arms and their supports, a splat, top rail and seat rails. The templates for that chair would be tied together in a bundle and hung high on the walls for storage in a cabinetmaker's shop (they can sometimes by seen in interior shop views in old prints).

Tenon
A rectangular or rounded projection carved at the end of a chair rail, for example, which conforms in size and shape to fit into a carved recess (the mortise), thereby forming the strong mortise-and-tenon joint.

Treen
The historic miscellanea of small wooden objects in daily domestic, farm, trade and professional practice, crafted by a turner. Most treen consists of one-piece objects; when of more than one piece, their junction was effected by means of turning on a lathe, examples being a lipped bowl and cover, and a stem threaded or dowelled and glued into a base, and thus were not joiner made. Objects intended solely for ornament, such as carved figures and panels, are not described as treen.

Trifid
Three-part foot of three lobes, also known as a drake foot.

Turnery
The craft of shaping wood by using cutting chisels upon a rotating surface. The device for rotating, or turning, the wood is called a lathe. Baluster turning results in turned members of various columnar shapes having characteristic ring, ball, spool, bobbin, etc., turned detail.

U

Undercut
A term used to describe deeply carved ornamental woodwork where parts of the carved ornament are separated from the ground or the molded surface.

V

Veneer
Wood cut into extremely thin sheets, or any thin sheet(s) of material, such as ivory or tortoiseshell, glued to the furniture core for decorative effect.

Veneering
The highly skilled craft of applying thin sheets of wood or other decorative materials to a surface. The purpose was sometimes economy and sometimes appearance, often the only way to practically display exotic wood figure too unstable to be used in the solid.

Vernis Martin
A generic name for a particularly brilliant translucent hard copal varnish finish (often called lacquer) used for the decoration of furniture and interiors in 18th-century France. The four Martin brothers, beginning as coach painters, developed a method and finish (patent 1730, renewed 1744) which brought them Court patronage and widespread fame. They used many colors but their green was the most famous.

W

Wainscot
Name originally used in mediaeval England for imported wood suitable for wagon (wain) construction, and thus for furniture and panelling, in particular.

Water leaf
A carved ornamental motif of a narrow leaf with regular horizontal undulations divided by the stem going down the center. It was used in the early 19th-century classical style and favored by Duncan Phyfe as a leg decoration.

SELECTED BIBLIOGRAPHY

Ames, Kenneth L., ed. *Victorian Furniture: Essays from a Victorian Society Autumn Symposium*. Philadelphia: The Victorian Society in America, 1983.

Bjerkoe, Ethel Hall. *The Cabinetmakers of America*. Garden City: Doubleday & Co., 1957.

Cescinsky, Herbert. *The Gentle Art of Faking Furniture*. New York: Dover Publications, Inc., 1967.

Chinnery, Victor. *Oak Furniture: The British Tradition*. Woodbridge, Suffolk: Baron Publishing, 1979.

Cooke, Edward S., Jr., ed. *Upholstery in America & Europe from the Seventeenth Century to World War I*. New York: W. W. Norton & Company, 1987.

Crawley, W. *Is It Genuine?* London: Eyre & Spottiswoode, 1971.

DeBles, Arthur. *Genuine Antique Furniture*. New York: Thomas Y. Crowell Co., 1929.

The Eye of the Beholder: Fakes, Replicas and Alteration in American Art. New Haven: Yale University Art Gallery, 1977. (Exhibition catalog.)

Fales, Dean A., Jr. *American Painted Furniture 1660–1880*. New York: Dutton, 1972.

Grier, Katherine C. *Culture & Comfort, People, Parlors, and Upholstery 1850–1930*. Amherst: University of Massachusetts Press, 1988.

Hayward, Charles H. *Antique or Fake? The Making of Old Furniture*. London: Evans Brothers Ltd., 1970.

——. *Furniture Repairs*. London: Evans Brothers Ltd., 1967.

Hewitt, Benjamin A., Kane, Patricia E., and Ward, Gerald W. R. *The Work of Many Hands: Card Tables in Federal America 1790–1820*. New Haven: Yale University Art Gallery, 1982.

Hinckley, F. Lewis. *Directory of the Historic Cabinet Woods*. New York: Crown Publishers, Inc., 1960.

Hoadley, R. Bruce. *Understanding Wood*. Newtown, Conn.: The Taunton Press, 1980.

Hummel, Charles F. *With Hammer in Hand: The Dominy Craftsmen of East Hampton, New York*. Charlottesville: University Press of Virginia, 1988.

Joyce, Ernest. *The Technique of Furniture Making*. London: B. T. Batford Ltd., 1970.

Kaye, Myrna. *Fake, Fraud, or Genuine? Identifying Authentic American Antique Furniture*. Boston: Little, Brown and Company, 1987.

Kirk, John T. *American Chairs*. New York: Alfred A. Knopf, 1972.

——. *American Furniture and the British Tradition to 1830*. New York: Alfred A. Knopf, 1982.

——. *Early American Furniture: How to Recognize, Evaluate, Buy and Care for the Most Beautiful Pieces—High-Style, Country, Primitive and Rustic*. New York: Alfred A. Knopf, 1970.

Kurz, Otto. *Fakes: A Handbook for Collectors and Students*. 2nd ed., revised and enlarged. New York: Dover Publications, Inc., 1967.

Macquoid, Percy, and Edwards, Ralph. *Dictionary of English Furniture*. 3 vols. New York: Charles Scribner's Sons, 1924.

Marsh, Moreton. *The Easy Expert in Collecting and Restoring American Antiques*. Philadelphia and New York: J. B. Lippincott Co., 1959.

Mussey, Robert D., Jr., ed. *The First American Furniture Finisher's Manual: A Reprint of "The Cabinet-Maker's Guide" of 1827*. New York: Dover Publications, Inc., 1987.

Rodd, John. *The Repair and Restoration of Furniture*. New York: Charles Scribner's Sons, 1955.

Sack, Albert. *Fine Points of Furniture: Early American*. New York: Crown Publishers, 1950.

Savage, George. *Forgeries, Fakes and Reproductions: A Handbook for the Art Dealer and Collector*. New York: Praeger, 1963.

Symonds, R. W. *Old English Walnut and Lacquer Furniture: The Present-Day Condition and Value and the Methods of the Furniture-Faker in Producing Spurious Pieces*. New York: Robert M. McBride & Co., 1923.

Williams, Marc A. *Keeping It All Together: The Preservation and Care of Historic Furniture*. Worthington, Ohio: Ohio Antique Review, 1988.

Yates, Raymond F. *Antique Fakes and Their Detection*. New York: Harper & Bros. Publishers, 1950.

INDEX